The Truth About Fiction

The Truth About Fiction

Steven Schoen

Mt. Hood Community College

Prentice Hall
Upper Saddle River, NJ 07458

Library of Congress Cataloging-in-Publication Data
Schoen, Steven
   The truth about fiction / Steven Schoen.
      p. cm.
   Includes index.
   ISBN 0-13-025771-0
   1. Fiction—Authorship. 2. Fiction—Technique. 3. Creative writing.
   I. Title.
PN3355 .S385 1999
808.3—dc21   99-051599

Editorial Director: Charlyce Jones Owen
Editor-in-Chief: Leah Jewell
Acquisitions Editor: Carrie Brandon
Editorial Assistant: Sandy Hrasdzira
AVP, Director of Production and Manufacturing: Barbara Kittle
Senior Managing Editor: Bonnie Biller
Production Editor: Randy Pettit
Manufacturing Manager: Nick Sklitsis
Prepress and Manufacturing Buyer: Lynn Pearlman
Marketing Director: Gina Sluss
Marketing Manager: Brandy Dawson
Cover Design: Robert Farrar-Wagner
Cover Photo: Steven Schoen

This book was set in 10/13 Palatino by Carlisle Communications Ltd.,

Printed in the United States of America
10 9 8 7 6 5

ISBN: 0-13-025771-0

Prentice-Hall International (UK) Limited, *London*
Prentice-Hall of Australia Pty. Limited, *Sydney*
Prentice-Hall Canada Inc., *Toronto*
Prentice-Hall Hispanoamerica, S.A., *Mexico*
Prentice-Hall of India Private Limited, *New Delhi*
Prentice-Hall of Japan, Inc., *Tokyo*
Pearson Education Asia Pte. Ltd., *Singapore*
Editora Prentice-Hall do Brasil, Ltda., *Rio de Janeiro*

To my wife Jan,
who gives it all meaning

Contents

Preface to the Instructor

A few years ago, one of my beginning fiction writers commented that creative writing was the only course she had ever taken in which students were expected to know everything before they started. It wasn't really a criticism. She wasn't angry. It was just an offhanded remark about a situation that didn't seem quite right to her; but from the time she made the statement, it troubled me, primarily because I thought she was right.

On some level at least, the approach many of us take to teaching introductory fiction writing includes the assumption that our students are already instinctively talented, that they are mystically imbued with an innate sense of good storytelling. But they aren't. The plain truth is that almost none of them have ever received any actual instruction in writing fiction. Certainly, two or three students in the entry-level classes will have some flashes of light, but the majority begin in the dark. Most of them stay there. It isn't fair, it isn't effective, and it isn't necessary.

Part of the problem is inherent in a system that starts by saying, in effect, "Write us a story and we'll all tell you everything you did wrong." Without any prior training, the students' work is bound to be flawed. As a result, the feedback they get is rooted in negativity. The advice is more critical than instructive, and the atmosphere is dispiriting. Many of them walk away from our classes discouraged and feeling talentless—and no better informed than when they enrolled.

Unfortunately, existing textual material doesn't help much. While there are several creative writing textbooks on the market today, most are academic about theory. Their authors seem far more interested in literary intricacies than in giving practical, process-oriented advice on fiction technique. They make extensive use of examples by Nabokov and Faulkner. Their indexes are laden with references to Joyce and Cheever, Austen and James—great writers one and all and wonderful food for third- and fourth-year English majors, but absolutely inaccessible for the majority of entry-level fiction-writing students.

The result is that most current textbooks dominate the classroom. They themselves become the focus of discussion, and student writing gets lost in the process.

Our students don't take creative writing classes because they adore the stylistic fine points of literary giants. They don't yet write at that level; and they don't yet think at that level. Such material intimidates them, and they are universally bored cross-eyed at the prospect of having to wade through nearly impenetrable material for a kernel or two of useful information. They already know that fiction is art. What they want and need is pragmatic advice—no-nonsense, entry-level emphasis on craft.

The Truth About Fiction is designed to give them just that. Spurred by my student's remark, I collected and studied over half a million student words. In revision, I did the same with half a million more. I kept a complete record of the problems the students faced and of all the marginal notes and instructional advice I had given to help them get past those problems. The idea was to address their specific needs with brief, straightforward, digestible discussions of fiction technique. If I could help them manage the most common writing errors *before* they made them, their work (and not incidently, their self-esteem and their interest in writing) would improve.

Using a logical and practical sequence, this book treats creative writing as a skill-building course. It supplements course content rather than engulfing it. From dialogue mechanics to point of view, from the essence of conflict to advice on how to build a person, each subject is treated in clear, manageable units which can be assigned both before class and during to deal with specific student problems. Its tone is personal and encouraging, its explanations and examples are clear and to the point, and its coverage is complete.

To stimulate class discussion, each chapter contains "Something to Think About," a collection of brief and challenging observations about the art and craft of writing.

You will also find a wide range of exercises, from the simple, such as emphasizing sensory language choices, to the more complex issues of causal plotting and stimulus-response character motivation. These can be used very effectively either alone or to build the students' abilities toward successful completion of longer-term projects.

What you won't find is long, involved academic essays on literary intricacies—just sound, simple advice on what works, what doesn't, and why. As one reviewer put it,

> Here in one little book is everything one needs to know about writing fiction presented clearly and engagingly. The book is lean and efficient. No fluff, no nonsense—everything is to the point. It made me feel that if I wanted to—really wanted to—I could write fiction successfully! I'm confident it would have the same effect on students.

Preface to the Student

One popular theory about brain function says your thinking style is influenced by whichever side of your brain is dominant. The right side is the creative side, the side that wants to throw off all the rules and just go crazy. The left side is the structured side, the mental accountant who sits on your shoulder and insists you play by the rules and not make messes. Most of us have such an internal critic—that fearful little left-brain voice that tells us what we're doing isn't good enough, that people will think we're stupid and no one will love us ever again if we don't stop right now.

The problem is that we listen.

The editor/left brain thinks that the entire story must be in place and perfectly thought out before we commit a word to page or screen. It's so afraid that we'll make a mistake, it won't let us start at all. If we don't start, we can't finish. And if we can't finish, we have no product. And if we have no product, we can't be judged.

Let me protect you, the left brain says.

In frustration, we fling the paper aside and swear we'll get back to it, promise with our whole hearts. But we never do.

Or we stall. People who want to be writers are rich with creative stalling techniques, almost always spurred by the left brain's need for order. Our pencils all have to be sharpened, or the noise from the other room has to be silenced, or the hundred petty details a hectic world incessantly spins out all have to be dealt with.

Order, our left brain screams. *I need order!*

It's no wonder we can't produce. The key to good fiction may be revision, but we become so intimidated so early about leaving an untidy corner in the finished work that we can't even write the rough draft. As a result, we have nothing to revise.

Here is the harsh news—the difference between writers and the rest of the world is this: Writers write!

The rest of the world sits on its duff and thinks about writing, or talks about writing, or sharpens its pencils, but writers write.

You must make your left brain shut up.

Tell your critic to take a temporary hike. You'll need it later, but right now it must wait for you down the road. Otherwise, the editor in you will carp at every minor error you make, and you will be unable to move.

Begin with notes. Random. Disconnected. Messy.

At first, it is vital that you simply write, as uncritically as possible. It doesn't matter what, as long as it's words on screen or paper. Just get it down—ideas, potential characters and plot twists, snatches of dialogue, names, gestures, descriptions, complications, solutions. Reject nothing.

No matter how much your left brain nags at you, don't worry about spelling, grammar, or punctuation.

Don't even try to organize. Later, when you are comfortable, you can start to bring it together in some rough order. What bits tie together? What actions and dialogues fit where? But for the time being, just write.

It's fine to play with an ending, but don't worry about how far away it is or how you will get there.

When the doubts begin to slink around the edges of your mind, when the critic that is always with you begins to snipe, keep going. Movement is progress, and eventually progress must lead you to a product.

Even when you are well into the first draft, whenever you become stuck again or your vision fails (and it will happen), keep coming back to your right brain. Take a sentence out and wiggle it. Play with your people. Babble awhile. If you don't know what the character will do or what she will encounter next, brainstorm. Speed-list possibilities.

Above all, keep going.

The Left Brain Speaks—Briefly:

Ultimately, in the process of good writing, the time will have to come for you to bring some order to the chaos you've produced. In other words, you must apply the rules.

Usually, this is where everyone bristles. Creative writers hate rules. We want to be the exception, to soar above such mundane things. We want to be free.

Maybe that's the biggest mistake we make—equating creativity with freedom. They're not the same at all. With only a little observation, it's easy to find people who are "free" but not creative in the least, because they don't create anything. Of course, one can argue that creativity shouldn't be shackled to productivity, but maybe that's why there are so many fakers and posers in the world.

In addition, if we are honest with ourselves, we must admit that not everything we think is creative. Most of the time, if we are too free, all we create is a mess.

Actually, when people complain that rules hamper their creativity, what they're really worried about is stifling their imagination. Yet, imagination can only be as stifled as we let it be, no matter what parameters we set for ourselves. The truth is, having to quote accurately and spell correctly, having to detail scenes and maintain a consistent point of view doesn't inhibit imagination. If anything, having to play by the rules forces the imagination to work even harder. Of course, maybe that's the real complaint. Some people just don't want to do the work.

The craft of writing consists of rules, from spelling and punctuation all the way to character and plot and symbolism. Ultimately, if you understand the craft, you will feel the rhythm of your sentences. You will have a dozen different methods to call upon to make your people seem real. Your dialogues will be crisp and tense. You'll know how to foreshadow, how to pace a story, how to intensify plot and resolve conflict.

In the end, writing is a public performance. If you only want to stuff your work into a box under the bed, there is probably no need to study craft or to learn to write better. But if you intend eventually to inflict your writing on an audience, you owe it to them to write well.

Something to Think About

- What keeps a chimpanzee with a paintbrush from being an artist?

- Good writing is often a matter of damage control.

- Many good writers succeed, not *because* they break the rules, but in spite of the fact.

- In the end, there may be only one inviolable rule in writing good fiction: Never be boring.

Acknowledgments

I would like to express my deepest gratitude to the following people for their invaluable help in making this book real: To Myrna Oakley, who taught the class that fired my writing heart again. To Connie McDowell and Stella Lillicrop, who shared their time, their work, and their always wise counsel. To Robin Reineke for her design advice, her impeccable taste, and those much appreciated writer's survival kits.

To Stacy Prock, who started the whole publication process and whose continued enthusiasm and effort gave aid at a hundred different crossroads. To Maggie Barbieri, whose initial editorial interest in seeing a revision made me want to write one.

To Michael Kelly, Slippery Rock University; Jon Gill Bentley, Albuquerque TVI; and Keith Coplin, Colby Community College, whose invaluable reviews guided me painstakingly toward the final copy.

To Carrie Brandon, who took up the cause and whose skill and faith made it all happen.

To Mt. Hood Community College and to my talented and dedicated colleagues for all their support.

And finally, to my creative writing students for twenty-eight years of inspiration. Thank you one and all.

— *Steven Schoen*

CHAPTER **1**

Lying 101

Basic Truths

Fiction is a lie.

Almost everything you need to know about writing successful stories starts with that premise.

A story isn't real. It didn't really happen. And even if it did, it certainly didn't happen exactly the way it appears on the page.

Okay, so fiction is a lie. But if it's well crafted, it doesn't matter whether it's a lie or not. Readers will believe it anyway. How many times, for instance, have you been angry at a villain, or hurt inside because a character was suffering, or laughed at a comic scene, or cried for a character's loss? Even though your logical mind knew it was "just a story," the writer pulled you in and made you believe.

The secret to crafting a believable lie is that it must feel real. All truly successful creative lying is reality-based. Even the alternate reality forms of fiction, such as fantasy and science fiction, find their success as a result of real-seeming details and real-seeming people with real-seeming motives. The characters' actions and reactions are what real people (or real slime-monster warlords) might reasonably do within the tense circumstances of the story.

The distinction is that fiction is only the *sense* of reality, not reality itself. In execution, a story is edited, heightened, manipulated. It is more tightly plotted than reality. It has none of the tangents and distractions that seem to plague reality. In other words, a story is not true.

Often a writer will want to tell a story that "really happened." The problem with that kind of a spur is that it is easy to become bogged down with the worry that you can't get it right. Someone who was there will complain that Cousin John arrived at the party after his brother, not before. And that spot on Aunt Vera's dress was soy sauce not ketchup; and after all, it really wasn't all that big, was it? The result of such worry is frustration—and ultimately zero production. It's far better to understand from the very beginning that you cannot ever be entirely accurate to life. Nor should you want to be. After all, the essence of fiction is the creative lie.

In a way, there is no such thing as nonfiction. Even biographies and books that claim to be historically correct have a looser grasp on real events than most people want to admit. The authors of those works have to reconcile themselves early to the need for embellishment and editing. They fill in details it would be impossible for them to know—the rustling sound of someone's gown, the calculating look in someone's eye, someone's quoted thoughts. They rewrite the actual speeches, because the real speaker got confused and stammered at the most dramatic part, or because no one at the time of the momentous event had the foresight to take anything remotely like precise notes.

In addition, real life is messy. The fact is, some real details do not fit well with a crucial mood. Or the timing may be bad. A seventeenth-century London love story would probably be ruined, for instance, by the smell of the open sewer wafting over the garden wall. The people of the time might not even have noticed it, but a present-day reader who is after a tender moment would probably be appalled. In trying to tell a believable lie, you are confronted with a world of real but troubling specifics that can drag down even the most spectacular "true" tale of war and passion. You cannot put in everything, and so you cannot be completely true to life. In other words, even nonfiction writers are forced to edit life. They must leave out the dull parts and enhance what remains. And isn't that how we define fiction?

Another factor which skews the truth is the myriad of language choices you face in every sentence you write. During that family party, Uncle Bob walked slowly across the living room floor. Or did he limp? Or swagger? Or stagger? Amble, shamble, stalk? Or any of a hundred verbs more powerful and more visual than *walked slowly*? Each creates a different picture and, thus, a different sense of Uncle Bob's character. But which one is the right verb? Which is accurate? You're the writer. It's your call. What mood do you want to create for the moment? What personality for Uncle Bob? What is the "truth"? Couldn't it change from writer to writer?

Fiction is also plotted more tightly than real life. Reality has loose ends. Accidents happen. Events stop abruptly or trail off incomprehensibly and without meaning. In reality, things rarely resolve themselves as neatly as we have come to expect in stories. In fiction, however, the author imposes order on all that chaos. Events are cause and effect. Actions have a clear stimulus-response relationship. Regardless of what "really happened," the writer gives the story's events reason and sequence.

Further, your characters are more clever than people in real life. As real people, you and I are forced to come up with those snappy comebacks instantaneously if we want to seem witty. As writers, however, we can take as long as we want to think up that perfect spontaneous retort. We can make things turn out the way we think they should have, instead of the flat, humiliating way they did.

Ultimately, what gives fiction a sense of the real is not so much its being real as its being reasonable. You should be guided by reality, but you should not be chained to it. Life should be the inspiration, but your story has the benefit of both vision *and* revision, something which almost never occurs in reality. Take advantage of the opportunity.

————————

On the other hand, fiction is the truth.

Editors, agents, and other authors are forever preaching to novice writers, "Write what you know." That's excellent advice on two levels.

The first level is obvious. You should limit yourself to circumstances with which you're familiar. For instance, you don't want to set your novel in Hong Kong if you've never been there or haven't done enough research. You'd simply make too many mistakes to be credible. Your readers would catch you in the lie, the worst thing that can happen in a story. It's better to pick settings and backgrounds you're acquainted with and to use the details you know to make your story real. While that may sound hopelessly dull, the best writing often comes not from exotic locales and characters, but from finding meaning in the mundane, from giving new insight into what others have overlooked.

The second level is a bit more complex: Write what you know *inside*, where the truth is. Write what you can be honest about.

In a recent interview, a famous author once mentioned that her eighteen-year-old son also wanted to be a writer. What, she wondered aloud, could he possibly know at his age about life that would equip him to write anything of substance?

The answer is this: He knows what it is like to be eighteen. He knows what it is like to be a young man who feels what he feels. Perhaps he even knows what it is like to be the son of someone famous who would wonder such a private thing in such a public forum. In other words, if he is honest with himself, he knows a great deal that might be worth hearing.

But only if he is honest with himself.

And that kind of honesty would lead him to understand what it is like to be other people as well, so that the characters he creates are not simply flat projections of himself, but real to him and to his readers, regardless of his age.

You don't have to suffer or to have had grand adventures or to have lived a long life in order to write well. You only have to be honest enough to see what you really are, and courageous enough to talk about it. Thousands of writers have written convincingly about death without first dying themselves. They do it by reaching down inside themselves and calling on what it *really* might feel like to die—not from television, not from movies, but from their own cores.

Writing what you know isn't merely plot and circumstances. You should write about what goes on inside you, where the truth is. And in the end, that may be the hardest (and most rewarding) work there is.

The Structured Lie

A **story** is an account of a character struggling to reach a goal.

In broadest strokes, that's about all there is to it.

In the actual execution of the story, however, we may want to consider some refinements to the language above. What kind of person is the main character, for example? Naive? Generous? Sad? What kind of goal is she after? What kind of struggle does she put up? Is the tone funny, or deadly serious? What language level should you use? What kind of narrator? The infinite possibilities are what fill the bookshelves of the world.

First, the character should probably be someone to whom readers will willingly give their attention, someone interesting. Don't make the mistake of thinking that "interesting" means the character needs to be a dynamic action hero with a buzz-saw wit and a thrill-packed lifestyle. It simply means the character should be someone worth the reader's time. With a decent goal and a little attention to heart, that could be anyone from bookkeeper to peacekeeper. Told right, everyone's story is worth hearing. The secret is to make us care.

Second, the goal isn't just any old goal. It is a *story* goal. That is, it's the single thing the character wants most out of the fight she's about to go through. Thus, it must be something of real importance to her, something that will improve her if she wins and bring hard consequence if she loses. After all, if the goal isn't meaningful to the character, why should it mean anything to the reader?

Third, the struggle should be complicated. The emotional impact is far stronger when the character must fight to win and when the winning is in doubt throughout the story.

A man wanted a new car, so he saved for a while and bought one. Where's the story in that? Where's the tension? It doesn't matter how snappy the writing is or how interesting the setting or how dazzling the hero; if there is no struggle, there is no story. Your readers should worry constantly that the character will fail and that it will hurt if he does. Make him need the car to care for his ailing child. Make him lose his job. Saddle him with fears and flaws and imperfections, and then use them to make the situation even worse. Create obstacles and villains so huge, so powerful, so disabling, they *seem* impossible to overcome. At least once in the story, particularly when things are going well, drop a failure into the mix. Then make your character fight to his feet and stagger on.

Finally, readers want to know how things turn out. They don't want to have invested all that time reading the story only to have it trail off into nowhere (or simply return to the same place they started). In the end of the story, you must resolve the conflict. But whether you decide to let the character win or make him lose, the resolution must come naturally from the story itself. In other words, the struggle must determine the outcome. It cannot come from any outside accidents or lucky but improbable events.

So "a story is an account of a character struggling to reach a goal."

Think of all the things you can do with that.

True Believers

There are two parties to the lie: the liar and the listener. Or in this case, the liar and the reader.

As with all successful lies, the audience requires serious consideration. For one thing, even before readers skim the title, they know that what they are about to read is fiction. So they are skeptical to begin with. Luckily for us, however, they are willing participants, asking to be fooled.

Still, that doesn't mean they are totally trusting.

Early in their training, novice reporters are told that in order to write decent news articles, they must scratch deep to find the answers to six fundamental questions any reader might naturally ask, not just at the beginning of the article, but as it progresses and after it is over.

Fiction readers have the same questions. When you first begin to formulate your story, and as you give it life, try to keep in mind that there are things your readers will want to know. You probably even know the answers. The trouble is, you won't be there to say them, so the reader gets ignored.

Try to remember the last time you saw a child struggling to say something important to an adult who wasn't paying attention. Certainly, your readers aren't children, but the frustration is the same. If you ignore them, they'll fume and walk away. The best way to acknowledge your audience is to anticipate their questions. As you plan and write, try to put yourself in the audience. What would you want to know? What critical questions would you have?

> **Who?**—gives the story its **characters.** Readers want to know who the people are, the relevant backgrounds and circumstances of their lives, their relationships to one another, their quirks and flaws, the force of their personalities.

> **What?**—establishes the **story goal,** the one thing the main character wants badly enough to suffer the conflicts and setbacks of the plot in order to get. "What?" also generates the goals for the ancillary characters as well, from the antagonist to the minor character who simply complicates the main character's day.

> **Why?**—addresses the **motivation** of the characters, not only in the pursuit of the story goal, but for every action and reaction along the way, no matter how small. What drives the characters to do what they do? Of the vast menu of possible actions, the ones the characters choose must have reason and must fit their personalities.

> **How?**—generates the **plot.** Once the main character and the story goal are established, *how* does the protagonist begin to move toward achieving the story goal? *How* does the antagonist prevent her? *How* does she deal with the adversity? And ultimately, *how* does she finally overcome the obstacles?

> **When?**—provides the story a time **setting,** a chronological frame on which to hang the events. Scenes don't need to be presented strictly in the sequence in which they would occur in real life, but the reader should clearly understand the time line of the story.

Where?—gives the geographical **setting,** in this case the circumstances and the sense of place. At the start, the world of your story is wholly new to your readers. Even if it is contemporary and generally familiar, the setting has important details that are unknown. If your readers are to empathize, they need to get a clear and early sense of the place into which they've been dropped.

If you can cover those bases, answer those questions before they are asked, the result will be a better lie, a more complete and satisfying story which draws the reader in from the very beginning.

Not incidentally, keeping these questions in mind while you write has the added benefit of helping generate more relevant material with which to fill all that intimidating white space.

Something to Think About

- Editors prefer having readers to not having them.
- Readers prefer happy endings.
- Readers are more attracted to stories about people who have empathetic motives and who do empathetic things. Thus, the villain main character is a harder sell. More interesting, maybe, but a harder sell.
- The best judge of whether the goal is significant or not is probably the character whose goal it is. Getting the north forty plowed and planted by the first rain might not seem like very much to some people, but it could be absolutely critical to the right narrator.
- Flaws make your people more real and your plots more complex.
- Speculative fiction, such as fantasy or science fiction, begins with the question "What if . . . ?" (What if we colonized another planet or met aliens? What if sorcerers and elves roamed the world? What if John F. Kennedy had not been assassinated?) Once the new reality is established, the characters imitate life as closely as possible within the rules of that new scope.

EXERCISES

1-1. **A Simple Start:** Write a list of ten descriptive synonyms for *walked*. Define each clearly enough to show how it is different from the others, and briefly describe the circumstances where it might be used. For example, *stagger* describes the slow, halting, perhaps chaotic walk of someone in pain or someone who is drunk or mentally incapacitated.

1-2. **Experience List:** What *do* you know? List five general categories of your personal experience. Try for at least two of your own, but if you're stuck for categories, consider these:

Jobs I've Held	Physical Experiences I've Had
Pranks I've Pulled	Relationships I've Been In
Skills I Have	Emotional Moments
Places I've Seen	Stupid Things I've Done
Places I've Lived	Injuries I've Suffered
Deaths I've Known	Strange Things I've Done
Beyond the Law	Other Settings I Know

Under each category, write at least ten specifics. For example, under "Settings," you might list cities, areas of town, specific buildings, specific rooms. These should be real experiences, not books you've read or movies you've seen. The idea is to list an actual knowledge base from which you might later be able to build characters, settings, plots.

1-3. **Fears List:** Write what you know? Ha! Write what you fear! Write a list of six of your fears, with a twenty-five-word explanation of each. Three should be physical fears, like a fear of spiders or dark places or the slime monster in the basement. Three should be more conceptual, like the fear of humiliation, the fear of poverty, the fear of losing security or love or control.

1-4. **Experience Quicklist:** A young mother receives a phone call from school saying her child has been taken to a hospital; a veteran space ranger loses his best friend to an alien attack. The scene is crucial to your story, but you have no experience of your own with being a space ranger or a mother, with losing a best friend or having a sick child. What do you do? For five minutes, pick one of the two situations, and quicklist some events in your own past that, with some massaging, might get you in touch with the emotions of the character. Why might writers have a hard time writing such scenes?

1-5. **Motives:** To all outside eyes, Dave and Myrna have been happily married for forty-three years. But one morning over a leisurely breakfast, Myrna suddenly rips the newspaper out of Dave's hands, wads it up, and throws it on the floor. Why? List ten possible motives.

CHAPTER **2**

Details

Sweating the Small Stuff

Success in fiction writing is the result of dozens of elements working in concert—plot, character, setting, style, point of view, even individual word choices. Plot and character are the dazzling ones, the ones most of us are drawn to. Naturally, we want to create fascinating people who do intricate and exciting things. But of all the devices and tricks in the writer's toolbox, **description** is the one we cannot do without. It is the fundamental building block. And mastery of it comes before everything else.

Some readers refuse to read horror fiction because it terrifies them or because they find it simply too gross. Others avoid thrillers and high-action stories because they don't like the violence. People are entitled to their likes and dislikes, of course, but an important perception issue is at work here: If fiction is a lie, that means it isn't real. It's just words strung together. In actuality, there is no such thing as violence in fiction. There is only simulated violence. But if the writer does the job well, if the simulation is vivid and clear, the lie can have as much impact as reality. Maybe even more.

The idea, then, is to bring the reader's senses into immediate physical contact with the story world. When the ghoul's face melts off his skull, or the warrior feels the agonizing fire of his belly wound, it is done in such vivid detail and with such rich language, readers are compelled to believe it is happening right in front of them.

Or better, that it is happening *to* them.

Readers are drawn into a physical world that makes them feel the pain or scares up the hair on their arms.

And make no mistake, the good writer intends exactly those physical reactions.

The genre doesn't matter. Readers who don't like horror will just as easily buy into good romance or historical or mainstream fiction—and for the same reasons. Its physical details make it feel real. They can touch the brocade of the contessa's gown. They can watch the light flicker in the hero's eye and smell the cold fog seeping over the land.

The principle is the same. Success lies in sweating the small stuff. Details, details, details.

Show-and-Tell

When readers read, they follow the same thinking pattern we all do in real life. First we observe, then we conclude. The order of thought is important. The evidence comes first.

Beginning writers often try to shortcut the process, however, by going directly to the conclusion. They use abstract language and generalizations in the mistaken belief that summary creates more of a picture in fewer words.

The estate was *magnificent,* with *beautiful* gardens *everywhere.*

The creature was *horrible,* so Jane was *terrified.*

Sam was *irrational, out of his mind* with *rage.*

The reality, however, is that words like *magnificent* and *horrible* are so vague and have so many different meanings, they really don't convey any picture at all. What can the readers see, touch, smell? How do they *know* something is terrifying or beautiful? Indeed, why should they take our word for it?

The counterargument, of course, is that such writing forces readers to get involved. But the truth is, they have no evidence and no physical reference from the work itself. How can they take part, if they have no place to begin? The harsh reality is that most of them simply get frustrated and walk away.

It is far better for us simply to describe the estate in sufficient specific detail to allow readers to come to the conclusion "magnificent" all by themselves. What is it about the creature's look that makes it so horrible? What does it do that terrifies Jane? What does it sound like, move like? In detail.

You should be especially careful when it comes to portraying emotional states through summaries. Rather than "tell" those states, try to show the causes for them, then show the reactions. What is the look on Sam's face? Is there a set to his eyes? What are his actions—onstage, right in front of us? And if the story is done from Sam's point of view, we can describe what his internal physical sensations are. That way, the reader gets a clear sense of the emotion. If you describe a frightening event in detail rich enough to actually *be* frightening, the reader will be much more prepared to identify with the character's fear.

The way to make sure the readers' judgments are accurate is for us to make sure the picture they get is the one we want them to have, not because they're told what to think in general, but because the writing is detailed enough to let them conclude it for themselves. We supply the evidence, an account specific and vivid enough for readers to experience it themselves. But then we must step out of the process and let the jury deliberate.

Readers aren't asking much here. They just want to make their own decisions. When we don't let them, we expose a crisis in our confidence. In effect, we're saying we have no faith in them or in ourselves. We can't write it well enough; and even if we did, they wouldn't get it. So we feel compelled to summarize emotions for them, to "tell" them what they should feel about a certain character or setting or event. The plain fact is, one of these sentences is absolutely unnecessary:

> She met him at the door with a glare that could freeze lava. He could tell she was angry.

Action

During action sequences, things happen quickly, but it is a real mistake to think they would happen so quickly the character wouldn't notice anything. To the contrary, in scenes that move quickly, you should probably lay on the details even more heavily. Here's the reason: In moments of high action, readers speed up naturally. If you leave out detail, they speed up supersonically.

To combat that, you need to resist your own natural impulses to speed through such scenes. Instead, slow down. Add a wealth of small details. If your character has slipped and is falling down the side of a mountain, expand the sensations of the fall: the grit under his nails when he scrambles for purchase, the wetness of the grass, the sound of the wind, the impacts, the sight of the edge of the canyon rim rushing toward him.

There is a significant difference between real time and reader time. A real fall itself might be finished in a second or two, so fast the character may not have time to react. On the page, however, it should take long enough for the reader to *feel* it.

Setting

While setting is often conceived of simultaneously with or even after the story idea, this early in the process, it makes a convenient place to apply some of the specific discussion of detail and description.

The old joke goes: No matter where you go, there you are. True, perhaps, but where exactly are you? For instance, the first question a person regaining consciousness is probably going to ask is, "Where am I?" In a similar way, it's useful to think of your reader as a person first coming to in the brand new reality of your story. It's a different world for her. She's dazed, disoriented, confused. What, then, does she want to know? And when does she want to know it?

The story needs an *ongoing* sense of place. Early in the opening event, and as you move throughout the story, you should season the action with sensory details to give readers the physical context, some sense of where they are.

Season the action. In other words, don't stop the story to do it.

It used to be that setting details were presented in a block. Nineteenth-century authors often brought the story to a complete halt while they regaled their readers with essays on settings and characters. The novels of the time often set the stage with pages of static description and exposition before the plot even started. Writers today don't have that kind of luxury. Today, setting isn't simply the backdrop. It is an integrated part of the story.

Contemporary readers read for the plot. They expect it to begin early and not to be interrupted as it goes. Thus the setting must be included while the action is going on. The characters will interact with their location and circumstances as they move along the plotline. If the room in which a character suddenly finds himself is stark white, have him shade his eyes against the harshness of it. And while it is still acceptable simply to tell us a room is cluttered, it is both more vivid and more integrated to have your character deal with the mess by picking her way through it. From the opening paragraph, perhaps even the opening line, try to blend character, action, and place.

It was just after three when Jenny's father told her to call the family to the table. Her brothers got there first, elbowing each other, giggling, scuffing the hardwood floor as they scrambled onto their chairs. Alyse, her older sister, came next. She paused in the archway, one hand stretched dramatically up the mahogany molding, but when she saw no one was paying any attention, she slouched to her seat where their mother used to sit.

More Than One Hat

While setting provides a physical framework on which to hang the story, it also deeply affects several other elements:

Characterization Setting can reveal personality, particularly if it is the character's personal space. For example, stuffed kitties and embroidered pillows mean something quite different from cigarette butts and day-old soup drying in a tin pot on a hot plate.

In addition, the way in which the character interacts with the surroundings tells us a great deal about what kind of a person she is. The character who is comfortable in a cluttered room is far different from the one driven compulsively to clean it. The depth of her reaction to the setting, too, is an element. In what manner, with what attitude, does she clean? Is she angry, exhausted, resigned?

Plot Setting can also drive the story by supplying motivation. In fact, in a number of stories, the setting is actually the antagonist. If a character finds himself confined in a squalid prison or stranded in a hostile forest at the start, how he reacts to those circumstances will set the direction for the story itself. If he is submissive, the story moves one way; if he is revolted or afraid or angry, it goes in another. The setting provides an important trigger to the character's actions.

Mood The emotional tone of the setting is also the emotional tone of the scene, perhaps of the entire story. If the physical details are dark and foreboding, for instance, the reader is psychologically prepared for gloom, woe, despair, horror. Ask yourself what the feel of a place is and what details and language will capture it.

Beware, however, of stereotyping or being too overbearing and melodramatic in your settings. It is entirely possible to have a story which contrasts with its setting. Romance, for instance, can flourish in the awfulest of locations, and lovely settings can easily hold some pretty scary stuff. Ultimately, you can create any sense for any place.

Empathy   A vivid setting can bring your reader into immediate physical contact with your story. A fully realized setting provides the reader an opportunity to experience the story firsthand, through his own senses, to imagine what it would really feel like to live inside the physical space you create. If the details you include are sensory enough—if you *show* how things feel, how they smell, how they look—your setting should provoke a physical reaction. If the place is dank and frightening, for example, choose the details and the language to describe them in a way that will guarantee the response you want. Get physical. If you do it well, it will be absolutely unnecessary to say, "And it was really scary, honest."

Using Familiar Places

It is difficult to write convincingly about a place you know nothing about, particularly one you've never been to, so there is a great deal to recommend picking a familiar place for your setting. For one thing, you know how things fit together. If it is a town or larger geographical place, for example, you know where the parts are in relation to one another. If it is a smaller place, like a hospital or a fast-food restaurant, you know what is significant and what isn't and which small pieces give meaning and depth to the place. In either case, you would know what would help to establish colorful background, and what would just be pointless filler.

On the other hand, familiar settings have a "down" side as well. One danger is that you tend to overlook crucial elements. You are so in tune with a location that you can easily take for granted the very things that give the place its flavor. Or you may forget to put in some physical details because you just assume your reader knows where everything is as well as you do.

Beyond Place

Of course, physical location is not the only kind of setting. In some stories, a temporal or historical setting may also make a big difference to the story. The time of day can affect mood, for instance, as can various seasons. And the elements inherent in your time setting may influence the plot as well. The plot directions you take in a wilderness survival story would be drastically transformed by switching from day to night, from autumn to winter. Changing the time period from contemporary to historical also brings in new elements, new details, new possibilities.

In addition, societal setting may be vitally important to your story. Different socioeconomic levels, for instance, different countries, different political climates, different acceptable behaviors. A character in conflict with his social environment can make a fascinating plot. The difficulty with societal setting is that it is often hard to convey without lapsing into too much exposition. Generally, you are better off to illustrate the social mores by having your character actively encounter them. He can then comment, or describe—briefly.

Something to Think About

- The schizophrenia of writing: Writers sometimes live two lives simultaneously—one that experiences things directly, and one that processes the experience, describes it, massages the language it might be told with.

- Probably 80 percent of what we know in real life comes to us through our eyes. The wise writer learns to play to that sense. Think of the reader as sitting on the protagonist's shoulder, watching what the character watches.

- Don't neglect the other senses. If you are creating a person that your protagonist sees, for instance, you might include what the person sounds like—the noise of his breathing, or his sounds other than speech. Is there an odor? How would he feel to the touch?

- Description is only a tool. Its function is to get the story out in front of us. The main purpose is the story itself. Do not fall in love with your detailing. And especially, don't stop the story for it.

- As fascinating as you may find the setting, particularly in science fiction or fantasy, your readers have come for the story, for character and action. You can't expect them to tolerate static essays for too long. Get things moving.

- Don't forget the light.

- If possible, use all five senses.

- Don't think that any place is "typical."

- If you can, visit the place. Take notes. And pictures, which you can post for reference while you write.

EXERCISES

2-1. **Engaging the Senses:** It's a hot summer day. A young man and his friends drive to a river, where they find a crowd enjoying the weather. A narrow bridge crosses the water, and several people are diving from it into the river. One of his friends dares the young man to dive, too, only from higher up the span. He accepts the challenge.

In five minutes, list some of the physical things he will notice during his climb. Try for at least ten. Twenty is even better, and thirty would be great, since writing that quickly forces you not to edit as you go. Try to bring in all the senses.

2-2. **Specifics versus Abstracts:** For each of the following character concepts, create a specific physical detail that would show the idea without abstracts or generalizations. Write it in a sentence, as it would appear in a story. For example: "The old man was sad" is too abstract, too telling. "The old man hung his head and wept" draws us more physically into the situation. Write just a single sentence, no motive or background.

a) strong	b) kind	c) imposing
d) sad	e) generous	f) angry
g) fastidious	h) impatient	i) irrational
j) loving	k) boring	l) horrible

2-3. **Places and Emotions:** Pick a space that is familiar to you—where you live or hang out, for instance, or some room you have visited.

a. Using a single adjective, write a sentence describing the mood you'd like the place to convey: "The restaurant where I work is depressing," for example. Or "Donna's kitchen is cheerful."

b. Under that, list five physical details you'd use to communicate that mood. Then list two you would leave out, either because they are not relevant or because they run counter to the mood you're trying to create.

c. Then put a person in the space. The person has an attitude: "Martha is angry!"; "Ray is nervous."

d. Write a short scene (150 words) in which the person moves through the room. Show both the mood of the place and how the person feels without ever stating either abstract outright.

For instance, Martha steps through the door of the restaurant. She walks to the counter and sits down. She plucks a grease-smeared menu from the chrome rack in front of her and snaps it open.

That's thirty-three words from beginning to end, and only the last sentence contains any specific details. The first two are too general to convey a real picture. What else could you insert to show both Martha's anger and the restaurant's depressive mood?

2-4. **The Intense Moments Journal:** Somewhere, spread throughout your life, you have had moments of great intensity, moments when your emotions were charged and your senses were alive, specific events that were pivotal to the person you have become. Pick six of these moments and write a scene of one and a half to two pages (350–500 words) for each. Try to relate the intensity not by telling us something was really scary or very sad or the height of ecstasy, but by showing it in enough sensory detail that it moves us to feel as you felt.

Keep the opening background to a minimum. Concentrate on the moment itself. To work toward some sense of objectivity, write all your entries in third person.

1 memory

think KT's piece

make it believable

Due Next week — ~~Friday~~

Wed.

CHAPTER 3

Character

Character-Driven Plot

Faced with the prospect of constructing a piece of fiction, most beginning writers wonder, "What should my story be about?"

While that's a good question to start out with, most of us find it doesn't take us very far. The idea for a story first comes to us unpopulated, or with only a general sense of the main character: The story could be about a mother who fights to keep custody of her child, or about a knight who battles an evil wizard, or about a boy who gets lost on a hike. But those aren't stories. They're only situations.

The stories don't come into being until the character gets life. While plot is crucial, the story goal is nothing unless we have someone interesting who wants it. So, no matter how important we think plot or action might be, or how fascinating we find the places and history and technology, it all collapses without the people. Readers may want to be entertained, but if the characters don't seem full and believable, no amount of flash and bang, slap and tickle, is going to make up for it.

The important question isn't what it should be about, but "Who should be in it?"

Who is the mother? Who is the knight? Who is the boy? Those questions will not only give us a more interesting cast, but they will also actually generate the plot and its complications. Not just a mother and child, for instance, but an unemployed, impoverished mother and her blind child.

Well-conceived and well-conveyed characters establish an emotional connection between reader and story, a connection that is at the real heart of why we read, which is to find out about the people, how their lives and hearts are different from and the same as our own. Whether it is Fluffy the Kitten's search for a loving home or the warrior-poet's soul-wrenching struggle for justice in a cold world, readers read to feel what it is like to be someone else.

For the duration of the story, they want to *become* the character, to sense what the character senses. They want to think, "That's what *I* would have done. That's what *I* would have felt under those circumstances"—even though they've never been in a similar situation and never will be, and even if their real reaction wouldn't be anything like the one they imagine for themselves. Or they want to say, "I never would have done that . . . but I can see why she might." Either way, readers want to believe they are reading about real people with real emotions and real reactions (even if the real person in question is a cat).

From Character to Story

Some writers talk about their characters' taking over, writing the story themselves. As weird as that sounds, there is nothing mystical about it. If you build your people well enough from the start, they *will* generate your story. For one thing, knowing who they are will tell you what they want deeply, what they would do to get it, and what would challenge them most. You'll also know the range of their responses. Taken together, that information represents the story goal, the conflict, the complications, the character's possible actions, and ultimately, the ending.

Thus, your people are the engines that move the story from character profile to plot to resolution:

1. **Using experience, observation, and imagination, construct a portrait of an interesting, believable person.**

An operative word in this crucial step is *person*. You're trying to make the character full enough to seem real, someone with a life outside the story, someone with a history and, if conditions will allow, a future.

Spend significant time thinking about this character—who she is, where she comes from, how she lives, what hurts her, what makes her laugh, what she needs.

2. **To establish the major goal, ask the story question: "What does my character want?"**

In establishing the goal and driving your character toward it, motivation is everything. The essence of conflict is that your character wants something she can't have. The greater the want, the more your character is motivated toward the goal, and as a result, the greater the conflict.

Whether the story is comic or serious, most wants are universal. We either want to have or to be rid of something. We want security. We want revenge. We want to acquire or to be free. We want to avoid pain. Regardless of the tone of your story, the character should be driven to act in pursuit of the goal—from page 1.

3. **Provide a considerable adversary, something or someone powerful that stands in the way or works actively against the character.**

The story is about the character's *struggle* to achieve the goal. If there is no struggle, there is simply no story. Similarly, if the struggle is too easy because the antagonist is an idiot or the protagonist is too super, the story is flat and uninteresting. To create tension, at the beginning, at least, the antagonist should seem unbeatable. The burden is to find a clever way to overcome impossible odds. Easy, right? Anybody could do it.

The antagonist can be another person, the environment, the self, or any combination of those factors.

4. **Set the character into action—and make her fail.**

If the character succeeds right away, the story is finished without any drama. And smooth, unbroken rising action, victory after victory without a setback, is simply boring, since there is no suspense, no tension. The reader never worries. You have to make the journey more difficult. Whether it be because of bad planning, unforseen obstacles, or a serious antagonist, the character should have at least one failure.

5. *Allow* **the character to react to the failure, then to keep acting and reacting until the issue is resolved.**

With each failure, after an initial crisis of confidence, the character grows stronger. She suffers setbacks but continues to renew her pursuit of what she wants until she either gets it or she doesn't. Simply put, that play of action and reaction is the heart of plot.

That the character is "allowed" rather than manipulated means that the character acts within her own range and is not simply the author's puppet. Each action is the next reasonable thing; and the resolution of the conflict, the reaching of the goal, comes through the character's actions and effort, not because of an accident that neatly clears the stage.

Where you start the actual written story is up to you, but having a well-conceived character before you write will help you generate the story line. In plotting, with each action and failure, you need to ask, "What would my person do now?" If you know the character well enough, the answers will be clear. Repeatedly asking and answering that question—how your character deals with adversity and why she does what she does—is the stuff that plots are made of.

Whenever you are stuck on what to write *about,* whether you are just starting work on the rough cause-and-effect plot outline or you are in the middle of the written story, come back to this character process. Knowing the character will tell you what should come next.

Issue-Driven Fiction

Every once in a while, we get the idea that we should have something meaningful to say, a **theme.** We want to send a message, advance a cause, show a philosophy in action. We want to make a point.

The danger in starting with an issue instead of character and situation is that often the issue overwhelms the story. Our point is so important to us we want to make sure it's important to our readers as well. Rather than letting the plot simply flow as it reasonably would, we manipulate the events too obviously to make them fit the message. The characters cease being people and become puppets and mouthpieces. The dialogues turn into speeches delivered from soapboxes. There is an underlying sense of our hand on everything, and the story mutates into a thinly disguised sermon.

Certainly, your character will face issues: Should she betray her friend, is revenge acceptable, is self-sacrifice the right thing, is she her brother's keeper? But those questions are best left to the character herself. Issues are important only as they enter and affect the lives of people. Based on the circumstances and on her own way of thinking, *she* will decide what to do.

In general, meaning is better left to critics and literary scholars. If you write a story in which the bad guy wins, that might, in fact, say something about the way you view life; but that ending should be the natural outcome of real-seeming characters involved in a naturally flowing cause-and-effect plot.

If you're compelled to write because you think you have something to say, write an essay. If you want to write fiction, simply try to tell a good story. Through characterization, plot, and resolution, your story will illustrate your philosophy.

Something to Think About

- Readers want to worry.
- When you're casting about for something your character might want badly enough, consider the three R's of motivation: *reward, relief,* and *revenge.*

- Reading, even if it is bad literature, broadens experience and, critics of "book learning" aside, better equips us for life.
- A story is the account of someone being changed by her experiences.
- When you're deciding how your character should react to any situation, don't limit the choice. At each plot point, try playing with the possibilities. For five minutes, write down all your ideas, no matter how wild they may seem. Shoot for at least fifteen options, then pick the best, the most interesting—not the most obvious.
- Oddly enough, trying to force your character to do something he doesn't want to do or wouldn't reasonably do is a major cause of writer's block.

EXERCISE

3-1. **Inside the Picture:** From a magazine, cut a picture of a person doing something—not a simple head shot or portrait. It could be a worker of some kind, or someone having fun at the beach, or a woman sitting on the curb in front of a dilapidated house. Bring the picture to class for exchange.

For the picture you receive in the exchange,

   a. Describe five physical things you can observe from the picture.
   b. List and describe five physical things which you can't see, but which you think would be consistent with the scene. What is inside the woman's house, for example.
   c. Write 100 words about the conflict this person is in (either in the picture or outside it).

Defining the Cast

Levels of Character

Primary is the protagonist, the main character who wants the major goal. Usually, the primary is the point-of-view character, the one through whose eyes we see the story and the one with whom we identify. As much as you would like to have a whole group be featured, it is better to pick one single person for the focus. Even in a novel which follows the actions of several separate characters, only one is the primary at a time.

Secondary are those with whom the main character deals in major ways. They include antagonists, second bananas, love interests, close confidants, coconspirators, and sidekicks. In novels, these characters may have chapters of their own, although usually not as many as the protagonist.

Tertiary are the key characters the protagonist deals with on her way to the goal. These are the people who are encountered for a scene or a chapter, but who do not play the major roles—the suspects in a mystery, for instance.

Incidental characters are the bit players, the people in the background, the executive assistants, clerks, washroom attendants, and crowd faces the main character observes and/or must deal with momentarily.

Choosing a Primary

Most often the choice for the main character is obvious. She's the one whose story it is, the one the central action happens to. But sometimes, the best choice is not the most conspicuous one.

When you begin with a situation, you will generally have a number of participants to choose from. For example, a woman discovers that she has a terminal disease. The first thought is that it would naturally be her story. But who else's could it be? What about her husband or boyfriend? What about her mother? Her father, her younger sister, her best friend? One of her children? Her doctor? The man she is seeing on the sly?

Can you see how any one of these people as a primary character would lead the story in a different direction? Deciding whose story this is will be another means by which the plot is generated, since the situation alone is not a plot. It's only a circumstance. Plot is the result of the primary character in active pursuit of the story goal. And since each character wants something different from what the others want, each generates a different plot.

Not to get too complicated, but it would even be possible to write the story from a secondary character's perspective. For example, the younger sister or the doctor would tell vastly different versions of the woman's struggle than the woman herself would.

Thus, your choice of **viewpoint** has a great deal of influence on the direction the story takes. Consider the following when you make your decision:

1. Who is the one to whom the main action is most significant? That is, whose story is this?

2. Who will your reader care most about? Who will generate the most empathy or sympathy? Which one touches *you* the most?

3. Who is the most reactive? Who's most affected by the crisis? Characters who aren't motivated won't act, and those who don't act are boring.

4. Who is best able to convey the events of the story? Once you have chosen a point of view, you are restricted to showing events only through that person's eyes. Try to make the narrator, then, someone who can best tell what happens.

In Latin, the word *persona* literally means "mask." In fiction, the persona is the face you put on, the person you become, in order to report the events of the story.

In other words, the narrator is not you, even if you are writing in first person. She is a seemingly real person sharing her experiences and reflections as they happen. She is someone with her own personality, her own definition of the world, her own logic, her own set of rules, her own vocabulary.

The fastest way to put a crack in your reader's belief in your story is to reveal your hand on the character's strings. If an interesting observation occurs to you and you'd really like to wax poetic about it, you must ask yourself if it is something your point-of-view character would be likely to think. If it isn't, either you must reframe it into terms your character would use, or you must lose it.

So, when you're trying to decide who the primary will be, part of the consideration is which mask you can wear most effectively, because once you establish who your point-of-view character is, you must stay within that character for the duration of the story. You need to see everything as that character sees it, to think as that character thinks, to report as she would report.

Other Cast Members

Unless your character is in complete isolation and his struggle is solely against himself or his environment, you will need other characters. Like all other elements of story, however, your side characters must be included for a reason. One danger of writing a novel is that there is so much room, we want to fill it—often with people of no consequence. Remember, you're not writing a phone book or a compendium of fascinating people. You can't just have characters for their own sake. In one way or another, each of them must contribute directly to the plot.

In the course of his pursuit of the major story goal, the primary character will encounter people who actively oppose him or who simply cause problems and complications. Others may support him or sidekick for him or aid his cause when he most needs help. Still others will be purely background, quickly detailed faces in a crowd, for instance, because without them there is no crowd at all. Or the receptionist with a bad attitude who stands between the character and the important woman he absolutely has to see. Or the waiter who takes his order in the Bavarian restaurant where he's meeting the man who will provide the solution to all his troubles.

Thus, support characters supply a stimulus which demands a response—most important because once the story is started, everything your main character does is a reaction to someone (or something) else's previous action. Without suitable and constant provocations, the story goes nowhere.

On any level, support characters add richness, diversity, and a sense of reality to the events. They also help to develop the main character, since, through secondary and tertiary characters, we get to see how he treats others and is treated by them.

Once you have decided to include someone, you should give her some sense of actual being. Whether you're writing a short story, where space is at a premium, or a novel, which affords a larger canvas, there should be a feeling that all your characters, from the primary to the most incidental, have full lives and personalities outside the simple frame of opening to ending.

Just as you spend time inside the persona of your protagonist, so you should briefly "become" your other characters as well. The amount of time you spend will, of course, depend on the level, but you should give significant thought to who your secondary characters are and what they want.

The Antagonist

The most important of the secondary characters, the antagonist deserves nearly as much consideration as the primary. It is a huge mistake to think of him as simply the "bad guy" or the villain. Such black-hatted stereotypes will keep your antagonist one-dimensional and more like a cartoon than a real person; and the plot will suffer as a result, since his actions and reactions will be predictable, perhaps not for their specific intricacies, but certainly within a very narrow range.

In a well-crafted story, the villain of the piece does not rise in the morning, wring his hands with a sinister, maniacal laugh, and cackle, "What evil can I do today?" He does not oppose the hero purely for the love of being mean. The truly great antagonist believes with all his heart that what he is doing is reasonable. He has motives which to him make sense. Whether they make sense to us or not is another matter, but we should at the very least understand why *he* believes them. That's why it is often risky to base your antagonist on someone you personally dislike. You may be so angered, so emotionally close to the conflict, it will be impossible for you to see past the simplistic, and probably inaccurate, motive you've projected. The truth is this: Bad people do not think they are bad.

So you must ask yourself why your antagonist does what he does. Why is he so against the protagonist?

Oddly enough, weak development of the antagonist cheats the main character of development as well. Without a strong and complex force to struggle against, the hero is never called upon to rise to his full potential. He need only put forth whatever minimal effort it takes to reach the goal. Such is the stuff of fairy tales, where a simple, clever action saves the day, but it is not the basis of good fiction.

To create and maintain tension, the idea is to make readers fear from the very beginning that the protagonist will lose. The stronger, and brighter, and more active the antagonist, the greater the fear. And the more the hero fails, the more nervous your reader becomes. So, at least initially, the antagonist should be stronger than the protagonist and, whether onstage or off, should be working to win.

All this may increase your workload, since you now have to be shrewd enough to figure out an ingenious way for the main character to defeat a clearly superior force, but the story that results will be tighter and the end more satisfying.

The advice above applies to the antagonist as an active character. Of course, antagonists need not be human or even external. In the case of survival stories, for example, the antagonist may be extremely powerful without even being conscious. And certainly, great fiction has been plotted from a character trying to overcome a physical or emotional flaw.

Minor Characters

Unless you are terminally rude or hopelessly shallow, you would never tell a real person he is only a minor character. When you are writing, you need to bring that same sensitivity to all your fictional people as well, no matter how briefly we may encounter them. You cannot simply have the waiter, the hotel desk clerk, the receptionist. No one, including your main character, moves through a neutral world populated only by mannequins and featureless cloth dummies. You must try to capture a feeling that each person, even a minor one, exists wholly before the main character enters the scene, and will continue to exist wholly after the character leaves.

By giving your tertiary and incidental characters a sense of personality, you texturize the landscape. The problem is that you have only a few sentences to accomplish the impression. If you use more, the reader has the right to believe the minor character is going to play a more major role. So you have to be fast.

Introduce even your incidentals strongly. Don't be afraid to exaggerate a little. Define them with a gesture, a behavior or tic that sets them apart, something at least mildly eccentric. Try tagging them with a distinctive physical feature. Don't overdo it, however. The idea is to make them standouts, but not stereotypes or caricatures. And should you decide to bring them back later in the work, make sure you bring back the same person.

Something to Think About

- *Persona* is also the Latin root for *personality*. What exactly do we mean when we describe someone's personality? Aren't we really just talking about his public mask?
- It is better that you become your characters than that they become you.
- If they're all you, they'll be too similar to one another. Make your characters distinctive. Make them contrast with one another.
- If the character is you, you may understand situations, relationships, and motives so well you forget to give them to the reader.
- If the character is you, you may not be entirely honest.
- The revelation of the character is at least as important as the story itself.

EXERCISES

3-2. **Character Responses:** Five people are in an elevator. Suddenly the elevator lurches to a stop and the lights go out.

    a. Give them each a name and a one-sentence background.

    b. List one physical and one verbal response each would have at the instant of the event.

    c. Describe how each would act after the first minute.

Try to create characters who are distinct from one another.

3-3. **Paradox and Quirk:** Each of these characters has appeared a number of times in print and on screen. It's pretty easy to stereotype them. It's a little harder to define them as individuals.

a food server in a truck stop	a cowboy
a third-grade teacher	a mom
a musician in a heavy metal band	a used-car salesman

| a construction worker | a judge |
| a gang member | an accountant |

a. Pick three.

b. Name two stereotypes, things people might automatically assume about each character.

c. Add two unusual things for each person. Make your quirks believable, and not too heavily ironic, since reversing the stereotype too abruptly is almost as shallow as the stereotype itself.

How to Build a Person

The Three C's

In the construction of real-seeming and believable characters—regardless of the subgenre of fiction you've chosen, whether it be mainstream or science fiction, horror or romance, fantasy or western—three rules apply across the board: They must be consistent, they must be complex, and they must change.

Consistency   The simplest type of consistency is just making sure you're writing about the same character throughout the piece, particularly in a longer work. In short stories, consistency is easier to control, but you still don't want the character to mutate inexplicably from one scene to another. On a physical level, the person who is six feet two inches tall with thick glasses in paragraph one ought not to be a four inches shorter and have perfect vision on page 10 . . . unless you're writing science fiction or fantasy and such changes are reasonable within the character.

Another type of consistency, even though some writers might bristle at the idea, is the necessity of keeping your characters true to type. As much as we all would like to believe in individuality, the truth is each of us is simultaneously both individual and type. As individuals, we may be wildly different from anyone else; but as types, we have great wads of attributes in common with the other members of our group. If we are loggers, we are like other loggers. If we are cyberpunks, we share interests with other cyberpunks. If we are elfin magicians . . . well, you get the idea.

Characters reflect a good number of the characteristics consistent with their "class," whatever that class may be. And while readers expect unique and interesting characters, they also want your people to fit at least some of their preconceptions. Their assumptions make them comfortable sooner, because they believe they already know something about the character when they first meet. Make use of these biases. If you let your readers assume some of the burden of characterization, you may not have to spend so much space developing what they already assume. And the space you save can be devoted to making your character more complex.

The third kind of consistency is internal. Each of us has a cluster of compatible traits that is the very heart of who we imagine ourselves to be. These are the essential core of us, the qualities and ingrained ways of thinking we will not go against except under extreme duress, if indeed we would go against them under any circumstance. A man donates a kidney to a child he's never met because it is in his nature. Another thinks that's just stupid. Our values tell us who we are and what is at our center. Their influence colors everything that we do. Our core defines every detail from how we dress to how we think and behave.

To any stimulus to which a character must respond, the range of her possible actions and reactions is vast, but it is not infinite. It is limited to those which are plausible for her. In other words, she cannot do what she would not do.

Complexity   Walt Whitman once said, "Do I contradict myself? Very well, I contradict myself. I am vast. I contain multitudes."

The same is true of all of us. While we may all fit into certain types, we are not stereotypes. We have an essential center, perhaps, but each of us is also a knot of paradoxes—a thousand conflicting qualities that somehow manage to coexist in the same person. Your logger might be devoted to his cats, for instance. Or your cyberpunk might provide loving care for his invalid mother. A fussy attorney can have bad teeth. A renowned scholar might be a country music fan. Similarly, the people with whom you populate your world should be based on both type and idiosyncracy. In other words, you need to include the quirks that make your character different from those who are like him.

The contradictions have to be rooted in reason, however. Whatever oddities or quirks your character may have must come logically from his background. If your logger plays with dolls, you'd probably better have a really good explanation. Throwing in weird quirks just for the sake of being different will not attract or keep your readers. It will simply make your people weird and unbelievable.

The character should also have flaws. Admittedly, the superhero can be entertaining, but the drawbacks of such protagonists usually far outweigh the benefits. For one thing, the character is too idealized to be believed. He's always ready with a witty retort. He is consistently brave and invariably resourceful. He never loses—and he's boring beyond belief. He's unrealistic, flat, predictable.

Worse yet, he has nowhere to go. If he's already perfect, readers know from the outset that reaching the story goal will have no meaningful effect on him, which means the story is a waste of time—for him and for them.

In the real world, none of us is that flawless. The inclusion of flaws makes the character more like a real person, and more like someone your reader can identify with.

In addition, even in its simplest form, a flaw can make the story goal harder to reach. For example, you've created a tough guy who has a fear of open spaces. For most of the work, he's indoors; but at the point in the story when he most needs all his wits to reach the goal, wouldn't it be more interesting to make him cross a field to do it? Think of the possibilities for tension.

Even more important, such complexities can also suggest subplots and story lines. Including a weakness, a shortcoming, or some internal war will obviously make the protagonist's struggle more difficult. Consider the impact of having to worry about a loved one on a character's ability to function, for instance. Your character no longer has a simple straight-line problem to solve. By making his life more complicated, you also make the plot more involved.

Change   A story is more than just the character reaching or not reaching the goal. As you build the character, you need to decide who she is, what she wants, and what getting it or losing it will do to her.

Whatever the character encounters in the course of the story must affect her in a significant, life-altering way. If what happens is so inconsequential that it has no impact on the character's life, why would anyone want to read about it? But if the situation is significant, the events must necessarily have impact and the character will be changed.

If it seems contradictory to ask for both consistency and change, you're beginning to understand one of the things that makes writing hard work. The simple, if somewhat confusing way to reconcile the paradox is that the character's changes must be consistent. That is, if she cannot do what she would not do, neither can she undergo changes she could not make. They, too, have to be within her range. Thus, when you're deciding how the events will affect the character, make certain the character's ultimate reactions are something she is capable of having.

Here, as in all aspects of your writing, keep the relationship between cause and effect firmly established. The changes your people make must be the plausible consequences of what happens in the story. The events and the personality of the character are the causes. The change is the effect. Nothing can happen by accident or simply because of the author's whim. Ebenezer Scrooge makes a drastic change of character at the end of *A Christmas Carol*, but Dickens has spent the entire work providing believable causes.

Character Files

If you were ever in a position where you could make a real human being and you wanted to do the job right, would you ever just make it up as you went along? Or would you spend some significant time first thinking about who and what you wanted the person to be?

A character file is a comprehensive study of a given character's background, from the physical details to the circumstances of the person's childhood, from the conditions at home to the deepest fears. For both consistency and complexity, some writers find character files to be the most effective method of building multifaceted characters. They help you know your characters so well that they feel like real human beings to you; and thus, they become real to the audience as well. While much of the information may never make it into your story, there are some real benefits to constructing files for your major players:

Motivations   An event may trigger the conflict, but it is your character's reactions that propel the story from then on. Knowing who she is, and why she is the way she is, will also tell you what the character wants. How she was treated by her older brother when they were kids may seem irrelevant to a current story about an advertising executive in a career crisis, but it could explain everything you need to know about why she'll do anything to get ahead, or why she always seeks approval, or why she hates men—and it could tell you what she will do next in the story.

Actions   Just as real people of different backgrounds react differently, so, too, will characters who are supposed to be real people. The character raised by circus performers on the planet Xerion will have ideas wildly different from one who comes from a family of environmentalist librarians. When you wonder how your character should react, go back to the file. What kind of person is she? What is her emotional range? Then decide what her next logical move will be.

Plots   As you sketch out the character's life, be thinking, too, about what she wants out of life. Try putting the protagonist in a situation where her current want is tested or thwarted. What could threaten her? What challenges her? What puts her in danger—not necessarily for her life, but certainly something that jeopardizes her emotional well-being. Give her a problem that is related to her file.

Complications   Granted, the primary conflict of the story may seem enough of a battle for the character, but that battle is made more interesting with additional obstacles to overcome. Give the character physical problems, for instance, or an uneasy relationship to contend with while she struggles against the main foe. You may even find that you have two or three plots running simultaneously. Admittedly, your task becomes more complex, but your story also becomes more interesting.

Backstory   Readers want characters to be real people, not stick figures. Character files give a sense that your characters had lives before the story started and that, circumstances permitting, those lives will continue after the story is over. In addition, the longer your story, the more interesting your character must be and the more you must reveal as the story progresses. If you don't know much about the character to begin with, you're doomed to a struggle to fill space.

Consistency   It takes far longer to write a story than it does to read one. During construction, you will have tried on a dozen different feelings toward each person and will have processed a hundred different ideas about all of their physical and mental characteristics. Some you reject, some you accept, and some you accept only temporarily. It's easy to forget. Character files help you keep track. As you write, keep consulting your records. If you change something about the character, track the ripple all the way through both the file and the story.

Maybe the greatest benefit of doing a character file is that it puts the character in your head, not just while you're physically working on it, but all the time. When you're eating at a restaurant, you'll suddenly "remember" that she lost her best friend when she was eight. In the dark of a movie theater, you'll think about how she wants more than anything in the world for her father to be well again. Her fear of dogs will jerk you up out of sleep.

Keeping a pencil and notepad close wouldn't be a bad idea.

Working Inside Out

Don't pull your people out of the air. The source of believable characters is experiences with real human beings—even if you're writing about aliens or grasshoppers. At least to begin with, use people you've actually encountered *and thought about* as your inspirations.

Your characters are composites, ideally drawn from two sources—outside and inside.

The first is the easy part. Simply go to places where you can observe real people without being too obvious and pay close attention to their exteriors. Study the people you pass on the street, those who sit across from you on the bus, your friends, relatives, acquaintances. Note how they dress, how they look, how they move, their shapes, their postures, their gestures and mannerisms—all their physical characteristics and quirks. You're hunting for tags and traits you can borrow to use later to make your characters distinctive.

The inside part is a little more difficult, and its success depends upon how honest you are with yourself and how willing you are to take the gloves off. But make no mistake, you must be good at searching inside if you ever want to write.

All of us tend to condense others with tidy generalizations and judgments that summarize whole human beings with a single impression: She's friendly, he's kind, she talks too much, he's a jerk.

But if we're looking for material, we can't afford such narrow squints. Real people are complex; and generalizations only rob them of definition. The character built around only one personality trait, or the character who is only extremes, only good or only evil, can never seem like a real person. Neither can stereotypes. They become characteristics instead of characters—little more than stick figures.

The cure is to discontent yourself with simple acceptance of their surface. He's kind? She talks too much? The question is "Why?" It's not just what they do or say or look like, but their motives and logic. Speculate about how they feel, what they think, what moves them. And especially what they want, because *want* is the seed of plot. The outside may be the starting point for your characters, but the inside is the source of your story.

As you create people and put them in stories, put some honest effort into imagining what it must be like to be them. What would you *really* think, feel, do, if you were set upon by aliens? If a homicidal maniac were chasing you through the jungles of Brazil? What if you had just lost a parent, wrecked a car, fallen into a river? Tell the truth from the inside.

For example, in a suburb near my hometown, two brothers had lived together for nearly their whole lives. They ate together, worked together, kept each other company nearly every waking minute. The only time they were ever really separated was when one of them went off to war fifty years ago. Then one of them died. How must it truly have felt to be the surviving brother? What must he have thought, alone at night in their house? What might he want? Can you see a story here?

Something to Think About

- Some people argue that the detectives in mystery fiction often seem flat. Perhaps it's because the detective isn't an active participant in the emotion surrounding the crime and has no personal investment in its solution. Thus, he or she is unchanged by either the case or its outcome.

The best detectives are those who are not simply observers and solvers, but shareholders as well.

- In general, reveal the flaw early for the protagonist and late for the antagonist. The early flaw gives the protagonist's struggle more dimension. The later flaw for the antagonist gives the protagonist an opening. Don't make the latter come out of nowhere, however.

- One overly popular ending among new writers is to have the main character sink back into her dreary former life. The problem with this kind of changeless character is that the reader has invested a great deal of time only to get nowhere. Imagine the disappointment.

- About the tedium of developing a character's background: Time is relative. While it may take considerable time to think out who your characters are, how does time correlate with quality? Jumping may be the fastest way to reach the ground from a skyscraper, but the quality of the end product may not justify the shortcut.

- If you don't know your people, how can you know what they will do?

- On the other hand, bearing in mind what great stallers we are, be aware that it is, of course, possible to become so enamored of the file process that you avoid writing the story.

EXERCISES

3-4. **Flaws and Complications:** List ten possible flaws and complications for each of the following story situations:

    a. A woman wants her invalid mother to live with her.

    b. A man must save himself after his small plane crashes on a mountain.

    c. A boy's father is captured by creatures.

3-5. **Character File:** Using the picture from Exercise 3-1 (or a character you would like to write a story about), construct a character file. List the following information, and more if you can.

    a. Physical traits: full name, age, height, weight, skin tone, facial characteristics, voice, mannerisms, health, attire

    b. Present circumstances: relationships, significant other, children, career, present social level, kind of home, friends, leisure activities, possessions, talents, affiliations

c. Background: kind of mother, mother's work, kind of father, father's work, siblings, relatives, friends, past social level, religion, schooling, military experience, travel, kind of hometown/neighborhood, achievements

d. Psychological traits: angered by X, jealous of Y, most loves X, most hates Y, addictions, sense of humor, phobias and fears, proud of X, regrets Y, strengths, weaknesses, self-image, secrets, most wants/needs X

For each category, pick one trait that makes the character's life more difficult.

Presentation

Once you know the characters' backgrounds, their physical traits, and their mental idiosyncrasies, the problem is how to integrate them into the story so they become as real to the reader as they are to you. Of course, your first focus will be with your primary character, but regardless of character level, the major development methods for integrating any character into the story are these:

How she looks	What she says
How she acts	What she thinks

Physical Description—First Impressions

No matter what your mother told you about not judging a book by its cover, you still do it. Everyone does. We measure, we infer, we generalize—instantly, on appearances alone, and most often with only the barest physical details to go on. On the other hand, and equally true, how we look on the outside reflects who we are on the inside. Like it or not, the clothes we wear mean something. The look of our eyes, the haircuts we choose, our possessions, our mannerisms—all of our physical features create impressions of us in those we encounter.

Such judgments may seem impulsive and unfair, perhaps, but their prevalence is a reality nonetheless. And knowing that puts you at a huge advantage in your writing, since, with just a few brush strokes, you are in a position to guide what your audience thinks of each of your characters.

The emphasis, however, is *guide*. Perhaps the most important principle of description is this: If you supply the details, your reader will supply the conclusions. Use specific and concrete language that gives a clear physical picture. Wherever possible, avoid judgment and summary descriptions entirely—*strong, gorgeous, imposing. At very least,* follow them with explanatory detail so the reader can see for herself.

But what details should you choose to represent the whole? Obviously, any real person is a mass of physical characteristics. It would take a book-length list just to catalog them all. You have to be more judicious than that, however. Even in a novel, the amount of space you have to set the reader's impression of your characters is limited.

Since the audience starts to work almost immediately, you must work quickly to ensure the impressions they get are the ones you want. Decide early what general idea you want the reader to have of any given character and choose the physical picture that will produce it. The character who sits with her knees together while she sips her tea will hit us differently from one whose black swastika tattoo stretches down the side of his neck. Thus, the details you include shouldn't be just any randomly thrown together collection, but must point the reader in the right direction from the moment of the character's introduction.

Later you can refine the picture. Be careful, however, that you don't leave out something pertinent. For example, if your character wears glasses, you might want to have him reach up and adjust them on his nose somewhere on page 1. If you don't mention them until page 6, it might run counter to the picture the reader has already formed.

It should also go without saying that while we might concentrate on looks, physical impression is based on more than simply visual information. The largest percentage, something like 80 percent, of what we know may come to us through our eyes, but don't neglect the other senses.

Actions—and Reactions

The majority of your story will probably not consist of blocks of setting or straight character description. Few contemporary stories can afford to be that static. While readers may read to discover about the people in fiction, they are kept reading because of what they are led to believe is physically happening in front of them.

Keeping that in mind, you should never entirely stop the action of the story while you describe or discuss anything. Instead, try as much as possible to keep your characters in constant motion, whether it is the hectic and dangerous action of a firestorm in a war or the simple gestures your character makes while talking to his invalid sister on the phone. People are delineated by what they do.

For example, the five people who react to the sudden stopping of the elevator in Exercise 3-2. While there may be a general statement we could make about how the five react, each one of them in the specific would do something different. One may drop to the floor. One may begin to weep or pray. Another may take charge. Still another might calmly call for help. In a story, every stimulus calls for a response. How your characters act and react speaks volumes about the kinds of people they are.

The smaller things, too, help to bring your characters alive. Their expressions and gestures, the individual styles of their movements, the physical things they habitually do are just as symbolic of their inner selves as any other external description you can present. Such small things are particularly helpful in presenting tertiary and incidental characters. The receptionist who snaps her gum while she talks, for instance, is clearly a different person from the one who taps a pencil impatiently or the one who refuses to smile.

Here, too, try to make your language as specific and dynamic as possible to convey the action. Don't settle for an imprecise verb like *walked* when more specific verbs like *wandered* or *minced* will give a much more vivid and effective picture.

Dialogue—How, What, and Why Your Characters Speak

Speech is simply a specific type of action or reaction, and like action, its performance represents the whole performer—his origins, his education, his attitudes, his sensitivities.

The pattern of a character's speech consists of the grammar, the syntax, the word choices and level of vocabulary, the manner of speaking and tone of voice. Your decisions about each of these elements for each of your characters will differentiate them from one another. "You want I should tell . . .," for example, conveys someone distinctly unlike the person who says, "Would you like me to inform . . . ? "

Equally important to characterization is the content of each speech. Faced with any stimulus, the character probably has a broad range of verbal responses available—all depending, of course, on the amount of character development you have previously done. Remember, just as the character cannot do what he would not do, so he cannot say what is not in his makeup to say. Thus, what the character actually does say under a given circumstance reveals what matters to him and consequently what kind of a person he is.

In addition, in every good fictional conversation or interaction, each person has an agenda. People do not talk simply to talk. There is *always* a goal, *always* something each character gets or wants to get, whether they specifically state it or not. Why do couples argue over trivialities, for instance, and leave the real issues off the table? Why do people make small talk on blind dates? Why do sisters in their seventies call each other every day just to say the same old things? What does each get from the conversations?

Real people are usually too compelled by habit or social constraint to say aloud what they really want or what they really gain in their exchanges. When you listen to them, if you want to know what the conversation is actually all about, you are forced to look for clues in the layers under their words, in their tones and subtexts. Cultivate the habit of looking for and cataloging those clues and their meanings. You'll use them later.

Dialogue is never just talk. The purpose is never simple. When your characters speak, try to decide what motivates each of them. It isn't just to give information.

Thoughts—The Voice in the Character's Head

Characterization by thought is governed by both amount and content.

In every sensory encounter, whether the character is smelling a flower or being shot at, part of her reaction is physical, part is mental. Before she acts, she first processes whatever has happened, then *decides* on a response. Depending on the situation and the kind of person the character is, the decision making may be deliberate and detailed or instantaneous, but it is always there. The amount of her internal processing you share with the audience determines the character type—cerebral or action heroine, or somewhere in between. That is, does she think about everything, or simply act? Even if it is the latter, make sure you leave physical signs that the character has at least some mental activity, like pausing or giving meaningful looks. (See also the section in Chapter 7 on Processing.)

In terms of content, direct thoughts are the closest, most immediate access you can grant the reader to your character. They are the means by which we see the world as the character does, not only through the character's eyes, but by sharing the character's attitudes and internal reactions as well. Obviously, the reader's task of discovering who the character is on the inside is made far easier by such direct evidence.

As schizophrenic as it may sound, the author does not tell the story. The character does. Thus, virtually all the details, even if they are supposed to be objective, will carry some hint of the point-of-view character's mind. The tone and the vocabulary will reflect the character's attitude. The details the character concentrates on will tell us what is important to her, what she worries about, what she is obsessed with, how she feels about what she encounters. Thus, we share both event and emotion, and the characterization is made fuller as a result.

The most effective presentation form for thoughts is indirect or even summarized rather than quoted.

Indirect:	She thought she would be sick.
Summarized:	She felt sick.
Quoted:	I'm going to be sick, she thought.

Each covers the same ground, but the first and second are somehow more readable and more acceptable. For one thing, quoted thoughts like the last example tend to sound a little artificial. They also break the flow of the prose, whereas the first and second seem part of an ongoing narration.

No matter what form you choose, however, make sure the character's thought is a natural reaction, a logical outgrowth of the physical story. Stimulus first, then response.

One final caution about peering into your characters' thoughts: The point-of-view character is the *only* person whose thoughts your reader should be able to hear. If you want to get into any other character's head, even if you are in third person, the only way to do it is to stop the current scene completely and to clearly start a new one with the second character as the point of view. Exceptions granted, that gimmick works best in longer works. And regardless of story length, in first person, you can't change heads at all.

Of course, it is still possible to know the secondary characters' thoughts without the ability to enter their heads. You do it the same way you would with real people—by careful observation of physical signs such as tone of voice, posture, attitude, and so forth, and by having your point-of-view character speculate.

A Side Note on Names

A great source of names is the phone book. Not much plot, but the cast of characters is fantastic. Also try the baby-naming books, especially if you want a first name with "meaning." Beware, however, of being too artsy, too cutesy, too manipulative, or too "meaningful."

Be aware, too, of the connotations of names. In your reader's mind, *Michael* has different meanings from *Mike,* for instance. Geoff is a different person from Jeff. And consider the tone of the sounds. Try pairing the tone of the name with the tone of the character. *Gary,* for instance, has a harder sound than *Gerald,* and a much harder sound than *Gerry.* The same principle applies to last names.

In addition, some names are no longer available to us because their connotations make them unusable, except for certain effects: Charles Manson, for example, or Abe Lincoln, or even John Doe. It might be a cute gimmick to saddle a character with such a name, but it's an artificial complication, and you run a huge risk of reminding the reader that it's just a story.

In general, try to make the characters' names distinctive and reflective of the effect you want them to have. Pay attention to the sounds. Try also to avoid both stereotyping and reverse stereotyping. And keep the names unobtrusive, yes, but don't make them so bland they're easily forgettable.

Something to Think About—Additional Techniques

- **Attitudes of Others:** What others say about the character and how she acts. In a third-person novel, it's fine to have scenes in which the main character is not present but is discussed, but in short stories and in first person, the protagonist is onstage all the time. You must set up a reasonable situation in which she could hear the opinions of someone else—by eavesdropping, perhaps, or by a direct confrontation in which another character lets his feelings be known. How someone physically acts around the character also reveals a great deal about how that character is perceived by other players.

- **Exposition:** Mini-essays about the character's significant past or present circumstances. Keep them brief, rare, and to the point, since they are not the current story but simply something to make the current story clearer. They are, in fact, summaries, shortcuts to avoid having to do the detailed work of scene and description. Sometimes they're necessary, and they move the story along, but readers relate far better to things physically immediate than they do to what is told to them.

- **Anecdotes:** Mini-stories. Everything about exposition applies here as well. If the story is somewhat longer and tends more toward scene than summary, it moves from the realm of backstory into being flashback.

- **Surroundings:** Where a character is often says a great deal about the person. The kind of house or apartment, whether she lives in a cell or a zoo, the kind of car she drives, her office environment. What does she surround herself with? What physical things constitute her comfortable (or uncomfortable) zone? Try not to be static, but have your character move through and interact with the environment. The nature of the relationship also reveals the person.

- **Similes and Metaphors:** These are rhetorical comparisons made between two things that have nothing logically in common. A love being like a rose, for example, or someone having a granite face. They're not meant to be taken literally, but to elicit a quick emotional response. Beware of being too cute or artificial or too obscure. Your readers aren't obligated to see the parallels, and there is always some joker out there who takes great delight in poking holes in the comparison.

EXERCISES

3-6. **Argument Dynamics:** Write a short scene (250 words) either re-creating or imagining a confrontation with someone you dislike or with whom you have actually argued, perhaps heatedly. Write the argument in third person, from the other person's point of view.

Use dialogue to show the substance of the argument. Use actions and descriptions to show the emotions. Use the narrator's thoughts to show the person's line of reasoning, emotional baggage, what he/she may have thought of you. Try to summarize the thoughts rather than quote them.

3-7. **Physical Traits:** Make a list of ten of your own physical characteristics, from your features to your carriage to your style of dress. Half should be those you came by naturally, and half should be those you have assumed. For example, your eye shape and color are natural, while your style of clothes is acquired.

For each, describe what you believe is the dominant impression on others.

For one natural trait and one acquired trait, analyze what causes the impression, how the impression might change from audience to audience, and whether or not the impression others get is the one you want.

3-8. **Character as Anathema:** Pick a character type you personally find repellent. Write a short scene (250 words) with physical context and thought passages to show the character in action. Make the repellent elements seem perfectly reasonable.

CHAPTER 4

Plot

Nothing New Under the Sun

If you want to make yourself depressed, all you have to do is go to a library or one of the new superstore book vendors. Wall-to-wall, floor-to-ceiling books and magazines. Page after page of fiction. Obviously, everything that can be written already has been, right? What new is there left for *you* to do?

Take heart. The fact is, in the broad strokes, on all those pages, there are really only six plots.

First of all, there are only three basic conflicts:

a. A person at war with another person.

b. A person at war with his world.

c. A person at war with himself.

And there are only two outcomes: either the protagonist wins, or he loses.

3 possible conflicts $\times$ 2 possible endings = six plots.

What, then, fills all those pages in all those stories at the bookstore? What keeps them from endless, looping repetition?

What accounts for the differences among all those stories is not so much the plots as the variations of ingredients. You could write a person-versus-person plot about a fiery detective hunting a serial killer or one about a humble nun fighting a slick drug lord in an inner-city slum. As far as that goes, you could even write about a humble detective drug lord pursuing a fiery serial killer nun in a small town in Iowa, if you wanted to. A woman warring with her world might be trying to save herself after a horrible fall down her basement steps or she might battle to change some social condition that she finds intolerably oppressive. The inner struggle can be with any of a million demons within—a shameful past, an obsessive behavior, a debilitating weakness. The conflict possibilities are endless.

If you really want to get tricky, especially if you are working on a novel, try bringing all three conflicts to bear in the same story. Three struggles simultaneously. Whew.

Add to that the variations of arrangement of event, of mode and tone, of style. You can use tight, terse prose, or you can wax poetic. You can be serious or play it for laughs. You can use long expository passages or high action. You can set the story in the future or the past. Then mix in how the individual characters interact and express themselves, what they feel like inside, with all the potential plot points in the character files. Now do the math.

Unfortunately, sometimes beginning writers look at all the previously written material out there and give up. Or they fall back on cute gimmicks or quirky situations or strange twists because they don't think they can come up with anything new without resorting to the bizarre. They confuse different with good.

Have a little faith. Don't get silly at this point. Just tell a good story about interesting people. The infinite permutations and combinations of character and circumstance and style will make your story unique to the world, too.

Plot Basics

As stated earlier, actual plot begins with character and goal. Something happens to shake the character out of her comfort zone, or she is already uncomfortable and wants relief, either through freedom or by gaining a possession. Whatever the goal, the character must want it badly enough to endure the significant problems you're about to place in her path.

The tension between wanting and not getting is called conflict. Without it, you have a plotless vignette. So there *must* be an obstacle, someone or something that stands in the character's way. The idea is to make your character struggle. Place obstacles in her path, make her fail, make her renew her efforts with increased resolve or skill, and make her keep fighting until the climax of the story, the final battle that decides whether or not she gets what she wants.

It is important to understand that if the problem is to be solved, the character must ultimately be the one to solve it—not an outside agency, not an out-of-control truck coming in from off camera and miraculously running down the antagonist, or a kindly benefactor we knew nothing about stepping in at the end to solve all the problems and set everything right again. It is the character's fight that keeps readers going. At the climax, if you take the solution out of your character's hands, your readers will feel cheated.

Finally, whatever the protagonist encounters in the course of the story must affect her in a significant, life-altering way. She must grow from what she goes through. If what happens to her is so inconsequential that it has no impact, why would anyone want to read about it? But if the situation is significant, and her fight to achieve the goal is profound, the events must necessarily have force and the character must be changed as a result. How could she help but be?

Cause-and-Effect Plotting

A tightly plotted story is a series of character actions and reactions, all devised through stimulus and response. It inflicts order upon the chaos that can sometimes govern real life—the cosmic accidents, the flukes of nature, or the carelessness of strangers. Such events may spark our characters' actions, but from then on, events must be cause and effect. The "inspiring" circumstance that starts the story, the initial situation that threatens the character's well-being and spurs her to act, combines with the character's makeup to constitute the first cause. The reaction she has to the circumstance is the first effect—as well as the cause of the reaction which comes next.

Therein lies the nature of causal plotting. What your characters do affects what comes next, and then next, and the downstream next. Once you set the situation up, everything that follows is in causal sequence, one action setting off another, which sets off another, which sets off another, each act being a reasonable (*not* necessarily obvious) consequence of something that went before, until we get to the end.

Motivation

One man's wife tells him she's been seeing someone else and wants a divorce. Another realizes that keeping his word will hurt someone he loves. A third has just been shot at or punched in the face.

What reactions will these characters have? What actions will they take?

Why do people do what they do? It depends entirely upon who they are and what they want. Fifty people may face exactly the same set of circumstances and do fifty completely different things. Each is a distinct person. Each has a distinct background and thus a distinct set of motivations.

For story purposes, think first in terms of basic, universal drives: fear of loss, the need for security, avoidance of pain, anger and revenge, or seeking pleasure—pursuit of a reward, for example. Whenever we act, it is because we want something. Your characters are no different.

Whether it be the larger movements toward the story goal or the smaller reactions to immediate situations, you should know why your characters do what they do. In its own way, motivation is the psychological setting, the mental background against which all the actions and reactions in the story are set. Motivation gives each action a context, a rational reason for its occurrence.

Some reactions don't need explanation, of course. If the character who is shot at responds by ducking, we hardly need the explanation that he fears for his safety and is taking measures to protect himself. What he is doing is simply the rational thing to do. The explanation is already in the reader's mind and doesn't need to be stated.

But what if the character responds by standing up, unarmed, and walking straight toward his attacker? We need to know why.

Supplying the motive for the point-of-view characters is fairly easy. Either before or during an action, you need only use the point of view to explain how the character feels, why he does what he does or is about to do. The character processes the stimulus and tells us how it affects him. Thus, you psychologically prepare the reader to believe that your character's action is the next reasonable thing.

Generally, it is less effective to supply the motivation after the action. For one thing, it has a sort of postmortem feel about it. That is, the action is over and you stop the story to dissect what just happened. Explanations are probably necessary, but the timing is not the best. The idea is to move the story forward, and such lulls stop the story's progress temporarily or, in fact, move us backward. There is also a sense that you have not planned well. It is as though you are saying, "Whoops. I forgot this important part."

Supplying motive for all the non-point-of-view characters is a bit more difficult, but not impossible. As you observe the other people in your life, don't you often speculate on their motives, question what makes them behave as they do? What clues do you look for on the outside to tell you what is happening on the inside? The same idea works in writing. You supply the physical, external clues, and your point-of-view character can speculate. Or your readers can. Either way, the idea is that you've left enough evidence to ensure accurate guesses.

The Next Reasonable Thing

One common flaw of horror movies is that the characters place themselves in jeopardy for a variety of stupid reasons. A sudden violent disappearance? A severed head in the parlor? The favorite reaction to such stimuli is to break up into groups of *one* and explore the creepiest, most threatening house on the face of the planet.

Why? Why would any rational human being do that? Not because they would normally do so if they were real people, but because it suits the director or the producer's idea of something sensational. There are possible realistic reasons, of course, but these films plot for flash rather than reason. When critics talk of thin plotting, unbelievable motivation is usually at the heart.

You should know, too, that movie and television audiences are fairly captive. They'll suffer through dreck more willingly than prose readers. After all, how many times have we watched something on TV simply because it was on and it was easier than changing the channel? On the other hand, all it takes to walk out of a story is simply to close the cover and never open it again.

If the character does something stupid, it must be a reasonable action for that character. She could be blinded by emotion, for instance, or be purely reactive, or even mentally unsound. Even mistaken is acceptable, but not stupid simply because it makes the action more exciting or artificially complicates the plot—or because you want them to do it. For a plot to work well, readers must believe the character would do what she does under the circumstances. "That's just the kind of person she is" is never sufficient justification.

Reasonability is not the same as predictability, however. In fact, often the most reasonable response is also the dullest one. Ask yourself the acceptable range of the character's actions. What behaviors are even in the realm of possibility? The range might be huge. Brainstorm. Get as wild as you can. Then cross off all the ones that are either outside the character's range or too predictable. Of the remaining choices, see where the quirkiest ones take you.

Remember, whatever the character does, it is your job to make it seem like the next reasonable thing. If the reader understands the motivation, even the most outrageous actions are credible.

Complications Set In

The road to the goal cannot be entirely smooth. As the story progresses, the protagonist's efforts will be challenged on a variety of levels and from a variety of sources. While the issues below are certainly large enough to build entire stories around, you should resist the temptation. Remember the problems inherent in issue-driven fiction. Instead, the issues can also act as motivations and story complications. In addition to the main plot, the protagonist is suddenly faced with other problems. A detective must solve a murder while battling racism, for instance. Or an ambitious district attorney wants to drop a murder case against a mentally challenged woman, but a corrupt newspaper editor manipulates public opinion to force her to pursue it. Or in order to fight to save the life of a bitter young addict in his parish, an old priest must face and overcome years of self-doubt brought on by a previous failure.

How might the issues below color a character's perceptions, influence her actions and reactions? How might they represent significant obstacles?

Bear in mind, too, that this list is far from complete. There are thousands of other issues a character might face in pursuit of the goal:

Revenge	Exploitation	Manipulation
Envy	Self-condemnation	Selfishness
Dysfunction	Self-doubt	Psychopathy
Doubt	Abuse	War
Hate	Suspicion	Perverted values
Fear	Failure	Rejection
Co-dependency	Greed	Abandonment
Sin	Pessimism	Unrequited love
Jealousy	Submission	Obsessed love
Bad judgment	Laziness	Addiction
Timidity	Bitterness	Unchecked ambition
Racism	Failure	Harassment
Crime	Denial	Compulsions
Public opinion	Neglect	Neglect
Avoidance	Secrecy	Caprice
Obstinacy	Deception	Compromised beliefs
Exaggeration	Defeat	Punishment
Corruption		

Similarly, when the darkness sets in after a failure, you don't want the character just to give up. She will need some reason to pick herself up and renew the struggle. Try these as motivations to keep her going:

Compassion	Unselfishness	Friendship
Confidence	Duty	Spontaneity
Morality	Equality	Preservation
Law	Faith	Honoring debts
Order	Affirmation	Keeping one's word
Sacrifice	Hope	Unconditional love
Commitment	Love	Higher meaning
Grace	Honesty	Truth
Fame	Dignity	Perseverance
Wisdom	Self-respect	Victory
Codes	Self-forgiveness	Freedom
Courage	Acceptance	Mercy
Growth		

Plot Outlines

When it comes to planning, there are three types of writers: the kind who plans out the entire work before committing a word to the page, the kind who doesn't plan at all because he doesn't want to stifle his creativity, and the kind who thinks he's the second type but needs to be the first.

Sadly, most of us fall into Type 3.

We're convinced that if we just start writing, inspiration will hit and the chain of events will drop magically into place. We wander through page after page, sometimes praying a direction will mystically make itself known before we've written our characters inextricably into corners and our plots have run aground. The sad fact is, we don't know where we're going and we have no idea how to get there.

Without a map, we flounder. Maybe we flail until we wear ourselves out and eventually the story dies. And maybe the next time we have an idea, self-preservation gives us a little stab in the heart to remind us of what happened the last time, and just maybe, we put the pencil down before the pain has a chance to hit us again.

While the argument about stifling creativity may have some merit, the plain truth is that most often we need a plan. One wonders if Michelangelo really started with a big chunk of marble and carved away everything that didn't look like the statue of David. More likely, he made numerous sketches from various angles, plotted stress points, tried on and discarded hundreds of ideas before he ever put chisel to stone. Even a genius needs to plan.

In an ideal world, we could spend great wads of time uncritically collecting thoughts about plot and character, sample dialogues, scene ideas, whole passages that we've prewritten when the inspiration struck. Then we could edit our ideas, put them into some sort of recognizable cause-and-effect order, and begin to write. We'd never have to worry about writer's block because we'd know exactly what to do next. We'd never have to worry about the internal critic's voice, because the structure would be so tight it would leave no reason to carp.

Everything would fit before we started. . . in an ideal world.

Okay, so this isn't an ideal world. But it isn't unideal either. Some compromises can be made. The plot outline doesn't have to be a full-blown, scene-by-scene (or chapter-by-chapter) scheme, even though we know that would make the job easier.

The least you will want is a good idea of the following:

a. Who the character is

b. What she wants more than anything in this story

c. What threatens her or stands in her way

d. What her first step toward the story goal is going to be.

Of course, even better would be for you to know how that first attempt works out, how the failure affects her, and how she finds the courage to continue. Then consider adding what she tries in her second run at the story goal and how that turns out. And eventually, you'll also need to know what her last act is and if it works or not. It begins to sound suspiciously like a plot outline, doesn't it?

Something to Think About

- Motivations: The reasons for us doing exactly what we do exactly the way we do it are rooted in our past.

- All acts have consequences.

- If you are planning a novel, try to think three chapters ahead of the scene you are working on.

- A story's central issue is its conflict. That means someone or something is in active opposition to your protagonist. While she is pursuing the goal, the antagonist is not sitting idly by, passively waiting for her to act.

EXERCISES

4-1. **Actions and Reactions:** A customer in a restaurant asks the waitress for a date. She not only turns him down but insults him as well. What does he do next?

For the next five minutes list possibilities, from small actions to large plans. Be absolutely uncritical at this point. Anything is fair game, no matter how weird it may seem. Once you have a good-sized list, say fifteen to twenty ideas, cross out all the ones that sound too familiar as well as behaviors your character wouldn't do or thoughts he wouldn't have. What's left?

Pick the most bizarre and write a short paragraph (fifty to seventy-five words) describing what would motivate someone to do that.

4-2. **Gender Change:** Repeat the exercise above, but change the genders. Are there significant changes? Why?

In class, exchange your list with someone. Are there any items on that person's list which clearly indicate that the two characters are truly different types of people?

4-3. **Plotting from Effect to Cause:** A woman's bitterest enemy comes to her begging forgiveness for something in the past. What did the enemy do to become an enemy in the first place? Quicklist ten possibilities. Pick three you like the best and explain why the enemy did each.

Cause to effect: How does the first woman respond? Again, quicklist ten possibilities. Would any resolve a story conflict?

CHAPTER **5**

Story Structure

Opening the Doors

No one likes feeling lost. At the opening word of your story, the reader, awakening into a new and unfamiliar landscape, wants to know exactly where he has landed and in what circumstances. One of the problems with a dialogue opening, for example, is that readers have no immediate sense of context. For the first few seconds, they're confused and uncomfortable, alienated from the story. That's why it's better to start at least with a sentence that establishes a picture of the speaker. Generally, on page 1 you need to take pains to give the reader some kind of anchor by introducing a sense of setting, character, and conflict.

1. **Where am I?** Set the scene. Briefly, what are the physical surroundings? Quick details or descriptions of setting will give the reader a sense of place. Try to make ongoing references to the setting as the story moves.

2. **Who am I?** Set the point-of-view character. Readers want to get involved, to become part of the story. Ideally, they will "become" the main character, living life as the character lives it, struggling as the

character does. Early introduction of the point-of-view character, the one through whose eyes and nervous system we will see and feel the story, brings with it the immediate sense of identification.

3. **What's happening to me?** Set the situation. Try to remember the last time you walked into the middle of a conversation and how hard it was to figure out what was going on. Readers don't want to fight their way to understanding. Don't plan on hiding crucial information in the hopes curiosity will drive them on. Just clearly spell out the circumstances, including the tension facing the protagonist.

You may begin your story with description, action, or dialogue (in medias res). Or you can start with a reminiscence, a philosophy, or narration (exposition). Regardless of the type of opening you choose, however, you must endanger your character early. It need not be high-action, life-menacing, breakneck-paced danger, but it must be a situation which threatens your character in some way. It must necessitate a struggle which, if lost, will cost your character dearly.

Even if you choose to begin with the action already in progress, you should stop somewhere on roughly the first page to establish the answers to those three questions. Through exposition/narration, tell the reader what is happening, how the ongoing action fits into the conflict, and who the major players are.

Better still, try to blend the explanations into the action as you progress, through internal processing, the point-of-view character's thoughts about the situation she finds herself in—if you can do it without making it seem artificial or contrived. The idea is to make the explanation seem like a natural stimulus-response thought the point-of-view character might have under the circumstances. The benefit is that the reader is immediately in the protagonist's mind and can feel what she feels from the start.

In Medias Res

In medias res is a Latin term which literally means "in the middle of things." Without prologue or explanation, you plunk your reader down with the action swirling all around her.

Note that *action* as it is used here does not necessarily mean karate kicks and gunfights, but covers all physical movements, from smelling a daisy to scrambling up a dangerous cliffside.

- Maria shivered in the dark room and tried to control her breathing. Her heart hammered in her chest. The wound on her back had broken open and was starting to bleed again.

- As soon as I stepped into the room, I knew I'd made a mistake. Aunt Rose set her teacup on the edge of the mantle. She had that look on her face like she smelled something bad, and even my brother turned away as soon as he saw me.

- "You will not speak to me in that manner," Hal Barber's mother said. She jutted her bony chin and stepped in close enough to see the pores on the counselor's nose. "I will not tolerate it."

Usually, in medias res openings have a better chance of hooking the audience because action brings readers into contact with the world of the characters. Instantly, they face what the characters face. If the action is engaging, the reader will stick around long enough to get his questions about circumstances answered.

It is a mistake to think that in medias res openings should be used for what we popularly call action stories, and that only exposition is suitable for the calmer, more literary efforts. The reality is that either opening is suited to any story. The first example above would probably lead to an action story, for instance, but the other two could just as easily lead anywhere. The choice of opening type is based on the style of the writer and the kind of impact desired.

Exposition

Beginning the story with a short essay about the circumstances prepares the reader for the story. By giving him the information he needs to understand what is to come, exposition lends a sense of familiarity before the action starts. Such background can include material about setting, a character profile, or even a philosophical discussion.

- In 1958, Squaw River was little more than a sleepy village at the wide bend north of Sutter on Highway 22. Thirty years later, it had all but ceased to exist. Moe's Canteen and the filling station were the only buildings left standing.

- Danny Tarbell was the meanest man in three counties, and he didn't care who knew it. He rode a lime green Harley with white and yellow flames on the tank, and he had a set of pipes on it that warned people for half a mile that he was coming.

- Some people are incapable of even the most rudimentary kindness. No matter what happens, no matter what face the world shows to them, their first response is to take. And no matter what the question, the first word to their lips is always a lie.

Clearly, exposition is "telling." If you do choose an expository opening, don't get carried away. Make setting the stage your priority; and when it's done, get out of the expository mode. You're simply trying to set up the story, the action, the *showing*.

Editors often give the manuscripts they receive only 250 words to hook them, sometimes even less. Since an exposition delays the actual struggle until the background is set, it is doubly important that the subject of the essay be fascinating enough or the style seductive enough to propel the reader forward into the story.

Notice that although the openings above may hint at the tension, the actual conflict will begin later when the main character confronts the problem. It is usually wise to get that going as soon as possible.

A Note on Voice: In most expository openings, there is a sense of voice-over narration, that the opinions don't necessarily come from any specific character, but from a disembodied voice that simply sets the stage. Once the story starts, however, and the point-of-view character (POV) is established, such statements should be the POV's, exclusively.

False Starts

Probably the most well-known false start is the dream opening, where the action seems to start, but then suddenly stops when the character wakes up. Readers usually find this especially irritating when they discover they've invested their time uselessly in a situation not immediately involved in the conflict.

Other false starts wander through a first scene fraught with attractive distractions, or catch the reader up in false trails and irrelevancies, while the writer decides the course of the story.

Often such openings are as the result of not knowing where you're going when you begin the actual writing. Some professional writers say they never have a plan when they begin, that they simply let the story flow where it wants, that preplanning only takes away spontaneity. While there is certainly much to be said for that argument, unless everything you write from the beginning is golden, you should be prepared to cut like crazy once the direction of the story becomes clear to you.

In a way, the false start opening is a kind of hoarding. You have worked so hard for every word, you are loathe to let any of it go—even if it no longer fits the story. If you find yourself not wanting to cut, try moving your extra passages into a recycling file. If they don't fit the present work, perhaps they will inspire something later. Don't throw anything away. But don't throw it into the story for no good reason either.

The opening should concentrate our (and the character's) energies almost immediately on the central conflict of the story. According to the principle of willing suspension of disbelief, the reader knows you're lying but has made a decision to trust you anyway. When the character finally wakes up or the *real* story starts, the reader feels tricked. Why would you want to risk losing his trust so early?

Something to Think About

- Readers will feel more quickly connected to the story if you bring the physical senses into play almost immediately.

- Generally, don't

   Start with a block of scenic description. It bogs the story down by stopping the action entirely and can be an intimidating way to begin. While fiction readers might also want to learn something, they're reading for the story. Get it going.

   Give more history or background than necessary. If it is necessary so the reader isn't confused, don't wander too far away from the story.

   Start too soon. Stories may move chronologically, but they don't have to start at the very beginning of everything. Otherwise, all stories would begin with the protagonist's conception. If you're writing a story of a maniac chasing a couple through the woods, don't start with them making plans on Monday of the previous week. Start with the chase.

   Open with a single character statically ruminating. The situation is ripe for a false start or flashback, neither of which is a particularly effective opening. If your character needs to think, at least make sure the subject has tension and the character is actively involved in some other activity while he ponders.

   Worry too much at the start about the exact ending. You should know the general direction before you begin, just to keep you from false starts and fraudulent trails. Readers hate feeling deceived. They like *being* deceived; they just hate knowing it.

- Absolutely don't use a clichéd opening, like an alarm clock going off or a phone ringing.

EXERCISE

5-1. **Story Opener:** Using the picture and the profile you constructed for Exercise 3-1, write an opening to a story. Stop at exactly 250 words, even if you are in the middle of a sentence. Have you answered the three questions that begin this chapter: Where am I? Who am I? What's happening to me?

Middles

A woman with a generally good life wants to get home to her husband so they can celebrate their anniversary. She leaves her office a little early, travels through traffic without any incident or delay, and arrives home to find her spouse, a limousine, and a bouquet of roses waiting. The happy couple dines at a wonderful restaurant, tours the sights in perfect weather, and arrives home mutually confident that this has been the best anniversary ever.

Boring enough?

On some level, this is probably a story, but where's the plot?

If you're trying to write a story worth reading, the last thing you want is for your protagonist to make an unbroken, bumpless trek from want to get. The beginning of the story might get us started by its excitement or at least its promise of excitement, but that won't carry us for long. If you want to create interest, you will need a plotline that challenges your character, one that demands she struggle toward what she wants, so that when she gets there, everyone is satisfied—exhausted, perhaps, but satisfied. In other words, there has to be conflict.

The Heart of Conflict

As previously stated, if there is no struggle, there is no story. Therefore, it's worth your time to pay significant attention to the central conflict of the story. For one thing, the tension and the story goal need to be *clear* at all times. What exactly does the character want? What force opposes her? What will happen if she fails? What does she get if she succeeds? The trouble should be spelled out early in the story, usually within the first 250 words.

Second, the danger must be *significant* in the character's life, a matter crucial to the safety or the wellness of the whole being. Make the loss mean something vital, not just a ho-hum return to a boring existence. If it signifies little to the character, it will mean even less to the reader. So the potential loss caused by not achieving the goal needs to be critical, perhaps unbearable. All of which should give a clue to your ending as well: If, after all the struggle, the character simply resumes life unchanged, readers can't help but feel disappointed.

Third, the problem's importance should be *immediate*. We're trying to drive the character into action from the start. If the dilemma is not an immediate threat, there is no urgent reason for the character to act or for the reader to care. Tragedy looming far off on the horizon does little to get us (or the character) worked up *now*. You should start your story as close to the moment of crisis as possible—preferably just before or actually in the middle of the moment itself, when your character is suddenly in need. Long expository openings that explain the circumstances often delay the tension too long. Readers just get bored. One benefit of the in medias res opening is that it starts with the peril right up in our faces, and that tension drives us into the middle of the story.

Conflict must also be *relentless*. A story is a series of **rising actions,** during which the character struggles toward the goal, and **falling actions,** during which she has failed and is dropping away from what she wants. In other words, she is always either fighting or recovering. The middle of a story can be deadly. You've grabbed the reader's attention with a snappy opening, and you've got a bang-up idea for the resolution at the end, but the middle flags because nothing tense is happening. Instead of being rising or falling action, the story is flatline.

Readers (and editors) aren't interested in long scenes in which everyone is content. It is acceptable to use summary to give your readers a few moments of pause during which they can rest, but when they do rest, it is always with the knowledge that the danger waits just outside the door. If your character lets down, feels safe or victorious, before the story is done, it can only be momentary and the moment must be broken quickly by another crisis.

The only time the conflict lets up for any significant period of time is at the end. Otherwise, you need to keep the pressure on. Whatever she tries either fails or makes her plight even worse. The worst moment, the time when your character feels closest to defeat, should come toward the end. That way you maximize the reader's relief when she finally succeeds.

Finally, the trouble must seem *insurmountable*. It must seem as though the character cannot succeed. Regardless of the type of threat, whether it is physical or mental, your reader must feel the character is in immediate and continual danger of complete failure. For dramatic tension to work, it is imperative that until the climax and resolution, the reader must fear the character could easily lose. Try to make the antagonist, whether it is another character or the environment itself, seem stronger than the protagonist.

On the other hand, readers like happy endings. In general, they don't want to have watched the main character struggle all that time for nothing. The tax on you, of course, is that you need to make the difficulty seem impossible to overcome, but you *must* find a way for the protagonist to overcome it. That's why good writing is hard work.

Problems, We've Got Problems

While the primary conflict should obviously be between the primary players, the protagonist and the antagonist, you ought not to neglect other hurdles as well. Instead of a simple tale of a white-hatted sheriff who wants to survive a gunfight in the lawless old west, you give him additional trials—physical hindrances, injuries, problems at home, problems with the town, problems with his emotions.

For one thing, if the protagonist is flawlessly competent and capable of everything, readers have little to fear, so they tend not to care. From the moment they meet him they'll know that all will be well in the end. While it may be entertaining to see how clever he can be, there's simply no tension. Instead, it is wise to build in imperfections and to allow your character to make mistakes.

In addition, besides being colorful background, tertiary and incidental characters can also serve to complicate the main character's life by giving information that changes the course of action, or simply by standing in the way. Not true antagonists, but more like minivillains, they are those forces in life that we encounter casually but which serve to set us back, or slow our progress, or thwart our schemes entirely. A short-term antagonist or two can do wonders for the middle of a story.

In real life, whenever we are presented with problems, we usually have a choice of solutions. In stories, while you should avoid the stupid choice which complicates the plot but which no sane person would make, you should also avoid the smooth path. In fact, it shouldn't even be an available option. Instead, try giving the protagonist two or three difficult choices, none of which is particularly attractive. To stay in his present circumstances is intolerable; to leave is equally distressing. If he chooses one reward, he loses on another level. By increasing his discomfort, you increase the tension.

For reference, return to the list of complications in the previous chapter.

A Note on Hope

In the face of all this downsided, failure-ridden plotting, you must hold out carrots to lure the reader on. With the usual exception of the final scene, all rising actions are followed by failures, during which the character's (and the reader's) hopes are tested. If the hopelessness is incessant, however, most readers will get depressed and quit reading. Therefore, you need to strike a balance, some note of optimism, even though the protagonist is losing at the moment.

Whether it is strength of character or that she has no other choice or the miraculous appearance of a fairy godmother, at the end of each defeat, you need to supply a reason for the protagonist to pick herself up and keep going. Whatever drives your character on will do the same for the reader.

As you plan, you should also be thinking toward a *reasonable* way out of all the trouble. Often, beginning writers tend toward tragedy not because they're naturally morose and prone to melodrama, but because they have written their character into too tight a corner and they can't figure out a clever way to get her back out. Tragedy certainly has established its place in great writing, but the *needless* tragedy is simply lazy writing, as is the other horror that comes from not having a reasonable resolution to a complicated problem: the accident that comes out of nowhere and simply wipes the antagonist off the map.

Something to Think About

- How many scenes will it take for your character to get from the opener, through complications, all the way to the climactic conclusion? Practice cutting, being efficient. Conceive of seven in a short story, for instance. Can it be cut to five? To three—before the incident, the incident, after the incident? To one?

- Often, the middle is the obligatory scene—the scene you absolutely have to have, because it is the one that most tests your protagonist's character and forces her to grow or change.

- Characters should remain true to themselves. If an action would complicate the plot but is a silly thing for the character to do, as much as you want to, you cannot have her do it.

- The choices the character makes should be irrevocable. If he can go back, where's the tension?

EXERCISES

5-2. **Complications Set In:** In the example that started this section, where the woman wants to have a perfect anniversary, what external problems might stand in the way? What might the world throw at her? What personal complications might she face?

List at least twenty.

Cull your best three and put them in order of progression in a story. Describe how you would lead your protagonist through her struggle to the end.

5-3. **Ever-Expanding Fears:** Using your fears list from Exercise 1-3, expand the list to twenty things that people (not necessarily you) might be afraid of. Again, no more than half should be physical, such as fear of snakes or fear of falling. The rest should be issue-related, such as fear of abandonment.

For two of each type of fear, write a twenty-five-word explanation of how the fear might get in the way of what a character wants.

Endings

An ending is not just where the story stops, or the point where you have run out of words. Endings must content the reader. After struggling alongside your protagonist for however many pages, the reader wants a sense of closure, a sense that the climax was worth the wait.

In essence, the final impression is as important as the first. We've all seen movies that have kept us entertained for two hours only to ruin the effect with a poor ending. Unfortunately, although perhaps deservedly, the net result is that we forget the overwhelming majority of good moments and remember only the final sour note.

The first duty of the ending is to bring the central conflict to a satisfying resolution, one that is warranted by the circumstances and brings the contest to a reasonable and definite close—win or lose. As stated elsewhere, readers want happy endings. You're not bound to that, however. If the natural outcome is that the protagonist not prevail, so be it. That is, after all, a rational cause-and-effect ending.

In addition, if the story does end happily, it is not necessary that the character come through it all completely unscathed. Changed, absolutely, but scarred works just as nicely—winning, but losing as well, which gives a sense that there are no easy answers and is particularly satisfying after a complicated struggle. In fact, too easy a solution is often simply boring.

Try to include a sense that the character has grown or been changed, which is a logical outcome. Most of us are changed at least a little by the horrendous things that happen to us. Something horrendous (the event of the story) has just happened to the character. How could she not change? Also, the changeless character is stiff, stereotypical, hollow, and uninteresting.

You should also not leave any loose threads. An ending should be a **dénouement,** a wrapping up of all the significant details. No characters left unaccounted for, no plot lines left dangling, even if you are planning a sequel. If necessary, you can include hints that there will be other encounters, but your primary job is to bring the present story to a satisfactory resolution.

Types of Endings

Event   This is the most popular, most anticipated, and probably the most effective ending. As part of the struggle, the protagonist commits an act which forces the moment to a crisis and brings the conflict to an end. Baltius finally confronts the evil wizard and defeats him. Sarah strikes out her tormentor.

Suggestion   The conclusion doesn't take the story all the way to its final moment, but to a point where the reader can easily see it coming. The survival story does not need to take the hero all the way to the hospital for us to know he will be fine. When the antagonist pushes the nuclear button, we don't need to see the holocaust to know there will be one.

Reversal   The protagonist realizes the goal he was pursuing is not what he wants after all. He might realize the error of his ways, for instance, or have a change of heart, or discover another prize is even better. While this ending has potential for character growth, there is also great danger of melodrama or sappiness.

The Ironic Twist   The character gets what she wants, only to discover that the prize isn't good or the struggle was unnecessary. Conversely, she might fail and be better off for it.

Epiphany   As a result of all she has been through, the protagonist sees in a new light something she formerly misunderstood. For example, the change of the character might be an affirmation that her way of life has merit, especially if there was some doubt at the story's start. Or she might finally understand another character or come to treasure something she previously took for granted.

Omniscience   Just as some stories start with a sense of omniscience before a POV character is established, some also revert to it after the POV has left the stage. It's an acceptable way to deal with the loss of the narrator, for example, but you have to take special pains to avoid moralizing or sounding like a voice-over narrator. Try to limit yourself to physical observations.

The Epilogue   It may happen that your character reaches the story goal sooner than you expected and you find yourself with significant loose ends, such as an important secondary character who left the stage in scene two in order to pursue a separate goal or another solution to the central conflict and is still wandering around out there when the story ends. What do you do? The best solution is to avoid the situation entirely by plotting your story more tightly. Barring that, however, a quick summary of how all the outstanding issues resolve themselves will get the job done. Still, the epilogue robs the reader of the chance to *see* those resolutions, and the effect is anticlimactic, since the high point of the story has already passed.

Chapter Hooks

Some students take a creative writing class because they want to write novels, or they already have one in progress. In fact, in my classes, the larger writing projects may be either chapters or completed stories. While much of the advice in this book is applicable to both novel and short story writing, there are some special complications when it comes to chapter endings. For one thing, because chapter endings are more like middles than final scenes, they should enhance the plot and deepen the conflict rather than end it. You need to force the reader to turn the page to find out what happens next. Try to break your chapters at one of these points:

> **A low note:** This is the most effective and popular of the hooks. If you have made your readers care about the character, they will be driven to read on to see how she will extract herself from dire situations or deep despair.
>
> **A high note:** Your character should have some successes, moments of celebration or relief when the character's spirit inflates. If there's still significant text left, the reader knows there's still time for a reversal of fortune and something bad is probably rushing down the street even as the character celebrates.
>
> **A sudden insight or revelation:** In the natural path of pursuing the story goal, the character comes across new information that shocks her or causes her to reappraise the situation. Readers will read on to find out the consequences, to see how this clue will alter her course of action.

An unanswered question: The character ponders the future, or the nature of the threat, or the intricacies of the situation. As the character wonders, so will the reader.

A hint of action to come: Action is always a draw. While it is ongoing, or if there is a promise of it in the next chapter, the reader will be unable to stop.

A point between the stimulus and the response: End in the middle of a scene, just as one character says or does something dramatic or just as a piece of action takes place that demands that the character react. Supply the response in the next chapter. (*Note:* If you are using multiple points of view, it is possible to insert a chapter from another POV and let the reader sweat out the response even longer.)

Just before potential danger: End the scene just as the character opens the door to a scary situation. Readers will stick around just to see what's on the other side. As with the stimulus-response hook, if you really want to play it cagey (and if you're writing in third person), don't go immediately back to the scene in the next chapter.

Loose Ends

As you approach the finale, you need to make sure all the little side conflicts and subplots are resolved satisfactorily as well.

> Our hero is seriously wounded in a plane crash on a rugged mountain. He and his less-injured friend are the only survivors. The friend decides to hike out for help. Days later, when the friend doesn't return, the hero resolves to drag himself down the mountainside. After a tremendous struggle, which takes up the bulk of the story, he emerges at the ski lodge parking lot. The end.

The situation is dramatic, the conflict riveting, the solution a reasonable outcome. But what's missing? What major question would readers still have? While it's not part of the actual struggle, every reader on the planet would want to know what happened to the friend.

It isn't necessary to place such wrap-ups neatly at the actual end. In fact, to do so may seem like an intrusive epilogue. Often, the subplots can be dealt with as the story progresses. The friend, for instance, could be discovered anytime during the descent, dead or hurt even more than the hero. The point is, after the reader closes the cover, it's too late to fix anything.

Forbidden Endings

1. Never write a first-person story in which the narrator dies. The reader's question is legitimate: If the narrator died, how did he tell the story? There are ways around this, such as using the journal form with an ominous last entry, or using present tense and cutting off the story just as the final danger appears. Both solutions are a little gimmicky, however, and the second raises a question about who the narrator is talking to.

2. Never end a story with "And then I woke up" or any of its variants. What greater feeling of betrayal could there be for readers than to have invested all that time only to find out the story wasn't real to begin with, that the character was never in actual jeopardy, and that all their worry was silly?

3. While it may be thought-provoking for grade-schoolers, mature readers detest the "Lady and the Tiger" ending: The story builds to a question rather than a conclusion. For loving a princess, a young man is sentenced to be eaten by a tiger. The princess pleads that he be given a chance—two doors, one with the tiger, but the other with a beautiful lady. The princess gets word to the young man that he should open a specific door. After internal struggle over her motives, he opens the door she suggested. Yes? And? Sorry, the story is over. You'll have to figure out how it ended yourself.

4. And finally, **the Most Forbidden Ending of Them All** (drumroll, please!):

Deus ex Machina

Literally translated, *deus ex machina* means "god from the machine." It comes from the habit of ancient playwrights so overcomplicating their plots it was impossible to wrap them up in a reasonable time frame by using rational cause and effect. The only way out was to insert a god character, lowered on a rope by a "machine," to sort out all the tangles and bring the story to a satisfying conclusion. The hero got the right woman, the villain was thwarted, all was right with heaven and earth—not because of anything the protagonist did to reach the goal, but because the writer took an easy out.

The modern equivalent is the accidental ending, the fortunate coincidence, the lucky fluke, the hidden strength no one had a clue about. The writer has written the characters into a corner and can think of no rational solution to set them free, so he brings in some outside agent to set things right.

Instead, the ending must come from the story itself. Even if it is surprising (and it probably should be), it must be a reasonable outcome of the events. It cannot come out of nowhere.

There is probably more to say about this kind of ending, but suddenly there's no need. All the writers of accidental endings have miraculously been struck dead by lightning.

Something to Think About:

- Endings in fiction are tidier, and more satisfying, than they are in real life, which does have loose ends and where actual events can trail off and be meaningless.

- Beware the ending that goes on too long. Frequently, a writer will come to the end and hate to let go. As a result, you may have five or six acceptable endings. Pick the best, and stop writing.

- In the same way that there should be no accidents, since most readers want a satisfactory ending that has the main character struggling against everything and prevailing, it is important that you build a character capable of success.

- Neither should the character miraculously find strength. That, too, is often a struggle—and a decent subplot.

- Readers want to see the resolution played out in front of them. Don't skip it.

- Include some element of surprise if possible, something unforeseen by the reader, but for which you have carefully planted clues. Just because the ending must be *a* logical outcome doesn't mean that it must be *the only* logical outcome.

EXERCISES

5-4. **Endings Brainstorm:** Using the survival story above, quicklist for other possible endings. Try for at least ten possibilities, at least three of which are not at all predictable. What circumstances would you have to build into the story to make the unusual endings work, and where would you place them?

5-5. **Reverse Plotting:** Reverse plotting sees the end situation and asks "Why?" Not "Where are we going?" but "How did we get here?"

Go to some crowded place—a restaurant, a mall, a bus. Watch the people around you until one of them does something dramatic enough to catch your attention. For example, in a coffee shop a young woman flounces into a chair and fumes at the person across from her. Or a man gets on the bus and stares straight ahead lost in thought.

Assume the action is the ending of a scene or even the end of the story. What led up to this point? Quicklist for possibilities. What is the person's emotional state? What caused it?

Write a short scene which includes the background and ends with the specific action.

CHAPTER 6

Dialogue

Mechanics

"I mean it, Ronny," Marvis said. "I can't stand it no more."

Her husband looked up from his newspaper. "Hmm?" he said.

"I hate that . . . that thing he does with his eyes. You know the one I mean."

"Yeah, I know, honey. I know. It drives me crazy, too. Looks at you like he could see right into you, right into your heart."

"Yes," she said, "that's just what I mean."

"Don't worry, baby." Ronny took off his glasses and squeezed the bridge of his nose between his thumb and forefinger. "It won't be for much longer."

Punctuation

"I mean it, Ronny," is the speech, which is set off from the rest of the prose by quotation marks. When the next part of the speech begins, after the speaker is named, it is indicated by a new set of marks.

Since the speaker is not part of the quoted material, the acknowledgment has to go outside the quote marks.

The connecting punctuation between speech and attributive is usually a comma, which goes *inside* the quote mark, and the punctuation after the attributive is a period.

If the attributive interrupts the sentence, as in the fifth speech above, place a comma after the attributive and simply continue the sentence inside a new set of marks.

Always use a comma to set off the person being addressed. There is a world of difference between "Grab me one, man" and "Grab me one man." Or between "Nothing, dear" and "Nothing dear."

The three periods in the third speech, called an ellipsis, indicate a pause. Had it occurred at the end of the speech, such as when a speaker is interrupted, it would have needed four periods—the last marking the end of the sentence.

Questions

If the initial speech is a question, it is acceptable to use a question mark instead of a comma inside the quote: "What are you talking about?" she said.

The more prevalent method, however, is to keep the comma and make the speech clearly a question: "What are you talking about," she said.

An alternative is to change the attributive verb to one that indicates a question, such as "he asked" or "she wondered aloud."

Paragraphing

When you change speakers, you must change paragraphs.

Dialogue should follow standard paragraph indentation, five spaces in at the beginning of the first line.

As long as one speaker is still talking, stay in the same paragraph, except if the speaker is long-winded. If the character is a speech maker and goes on uninterrupted by description or action or another speaker, it is perfectly acceptable to use a new paragraph (beginning with quotation marks) when the speaker changes focus. In that case, put the closing quote mark only at the end of the final paragraph, when the speaker is actually finished.

Attributives and Beats

An **attributive** credits the speech to the person who said it. A **beat** is a piece of action, description, or internal processing for the speaker, which also indicates who is talking. The second paragraph in the example above contains both an attributive (*he said*) and a beat (*Her husband looked up from his news-*

paper). Mechanically, either one alone would suffice to show who the speaker is, and sometimes you can do without any. Paragraph six, for instance, contains no attributive at all.

Beats and attributives can be placed at the beginning, middle, or end of a speech. Don't use more than one place in the same speech paragraph, however. One restriction on placement in the middle is that the beat should not be so long the reader forgets the initial part of the monologue. You should also keep all the beat material for one paragraph together. That is, once you've placed the beat at the beginning or middle of the speech, don't expect to give more when the speech is done. If more material is necessary, put it in a new paragraph.

Conversely, don't bury dialogue. Speeches can go at the beginning or at the end of a paragraph, or both, but they should *never* be buried in the middle, since the reader tends to lose them.

Make certain the attributive action actually describes speech. In " 'Whoa,' he grinned," *grinned* is not a speech verb. It's a beat, and so should be treated in a separate sentence: "Whoa." He grinned.

Thought Options

Generally the thoughts of the point-of-view character are simply presented as narration, not actual thoughts, but observations as they would be put by the narrator (*not* by the author).

> He watched her cross the room. She was something to look at, all right. Tall and lean, the way he liked them, and she had a look in her eye that told him she knew he was watching. If she looked his way, he'd lose it.

The preferred method of conveying actual thoughts is to summarize them:

> He watched her cross the room and thought if she looked his way he'd lose it.

The less popular alternatives are some form of quote:

> Quoted, like dialogue: "If she looks my way, I'll lose, it," he thought.
> Quoted, but without the quotation marks: If she looks my way, I'll lose it, he thought.
> Italicized: He studied her as she crossed the room. *If she looks my way, I'll lose it.*

Dialogue Style

Real Speech

The idea of dialogue is not to capture real speech, but to capture the illusion of real speech.

First of all, lighten up. If you listen to actual speech patterns, you'll find that most people rarely conform strictly to conventions of grammar. Instead, our conversations are full of contractions, imperfect constructions, fragment sentences, slang, and informal language. Tight mechanical control over your characters' words only makes them seem stiff and unrealistic.

On the other hand, some realities don't play well on paper. Certainly, real speech is loaded with pauses, with stammers and false starts, but story dialogue needs to be more essential than that. Do away with the ums, and ers, and uhs that plague us when we talk. Used sparingly, one or two might characterize a speaker or show hesitation, but make sure the effect can't be better achieved with a beat or a description.

The style of speech should also conform to the speaker's character. Although it may be pandering to stereotype, readers are jarred when someone from the streets speaks with an upper-class vocabulary and syntax. If you want to go against type, be prepared to explain the aberration in exposition or narration (or dialogue). Although real people often run counter to our expectations, your goal is only to make the dialogue seem real.

One pertinent reality is that in real life people are rarely tolerant of preaching outside the pulpit. They hate long speeches. You may be enamored of a character's words, but his listeners, whether they are other characters or your readers, probably won't be. How much can they take? A good rule of thumb is to limit your characters to four or five lines of actual spoken words, before someone or something interrupts. To break up the sermon, use a combination of beats, attitudes, descriptions, attributives, actions, gestures, and especially replies. This is dialogue, remember, not monologue.

Just as with other action-reaction or stimulus-response relationships, what one character says drives the second character to respond, whether it be through more dialogue, action, or thought (if it is the POV). If you're stuck with where to go next, look back at the last words someone said, the stimulus someone just provided.

Types of Dialogue

Direct: "I can't stand it," she said. "I'd rather die."

Quotes the exact words of a conversation. Direct dialogue gives the scene immediacy, as though we are eavesdropping or taking actual part.

Indirect: He told her she was wrong about everything.

The essence of longer speeches, but not the exact words. Used within scenes to compress the chitchat of normal conversation and to move quickly to the more important quotes or actions.

Summarized: They talked quietly for another hour.

A broad statement about the nature of a conversation. Used to provide background or as transition from one scene or scene element to another. Eliminates all but the most general sense.

Interior Monologue: He glared at her. Why couldn't she just keep her big mouth shut, he wondered. Always going on and on and on. Always about nothing.

Exact thoughts, as though we are inside the character's head. Note that if the narrator is clearly established, it is unnecessary either to quote or attribute the thought. The reader will know whose it is and that it is internal.

Attributives, He *Said*

The sole purpose of simple attributives is to give credit so the reader will know who is speaking. If you try to put more weight on them than that, they will collapse.

When beginning writers write dialogue, they often search desperately for suitable synonyms for the word said in a mistaken attempt to give their writing variety or style or, worse, dramatic flair. He rejoined, she asserted, the prophet harangued, the surgeon blustered. While the goal may be worthy, the net effect is usually artificial sounding or too theatrical. You are far better off simplifying. The attributive is the last place to show how clever you are with words. Let the action and beats carry the drama. The speech verb of choice is said . . . and said alone.

One reason is that while *said* is not the most frequently used word in the English language, it is probably the most overlooked. It does its work almost invisibly, which is what you want with a simple attributive. That is, it just tells readers who is speaking. They make note of the person speaking, then skip the verb—unless it is unusual, in which case the speech verb also notifies readers that a writer is hard at work behind the scenes. It reminds them that the story they're trying to buy into is not real life, that they are reading a lie.

If you tire of using *said*, try leaving off the attributive. Often, context alone identifies the speaker, such as when two characters are arguing. Even if it is simply a discussion, however, the characters should be sufficiently different and the content of the remarks distinct enough to tell us who is saying what. Make sure, though, that what is clear to you is also clear to your reader. We've all run across an unattributed speech and had to count back every other one to see whose words they were.

Another means of avoiding said, and probably the best, is to describe the voice or the character or to tag the speaker with a physical description or piece of action:

> "I don't think we're going to make it." Jesse's face was slick with sweat. He tried to smile, but the effort looked pale and flickered out before he could fix the look in place.

Beware, too, of the weighty adverb, as in Sarah said nervously. While such emotional shorthand is probably impossible to avoid, particularly when you are trying to move the passage quickly, try to remember the first rule of fiction: We all relate better to what we are shown. It's far better to describe the character or her tone of voice, or to have her take an action or make a gesture that conveys her nervousness.

If you really are driven to colorize your language, try not to force it. At least use verbs that are easily recognized and considered part of a normal vocabulary. *Replied* and *asked* are fair speech verbs, for instance, while *shouted* and *screamed* are acceptable. *Harangued* and *retorted* begin to cross the line, and anything odder or more dramatic is probably a bad idea.

The Physical Frame—Beats and Action

As mentioned above, beats and physical action are probably the best way of attributing speech.

For one thing, beats reveal each person's state of mind or personality. Rather than telling the mood of all the characters (which is a point-of-view violation), show those moods while they speak. In real life, when you want to let someone know how you're feeling without telling him directly, how do you do it? Through gesture, through silences and attitudes, through body language and posture, through physical action, you let your readers understand how your characters feel about what is being said, about their circumstances, and about each other.

In addition, beats keep the visual sense of fiction and help to prevent the disaster of talking heads, dialogue in which it seems as if no one is moving or gesturing or doing anything at all. The people become stick figures or hand puppets. If you engage all your speakers in action, even the smallest of things—picking lint, running a finger around the rim of a teacup, squinting into the sun, anything—you make them physically apparent to the readers. We not only hear the conversation, but watch it take place at the same time.

Beats also add realism to the sense of time passing. In an early beat, you can set some ongoing process in motion. The character might light a cigarette, for instance. As the conversation and summaries take place, the beats include her smoking it, then later stubbing it out.

As you plan your scenes, visualize the setting in terms of how the characters might interact with their surroundings. Think in terms of furniture, implements, odors, textures, colors, tastes, accouterments. Make your characters act and react during their conversations. Utilize postures, gestures, styles of movements. Someone might keep snapping his gum, for instance, or fiddle distractedly with a napkin. Another might not meet your eyes when she speaks, or duck her head when you speak. Someone else wipes his mouth repeatedly, or sighs heavily.

Beware: As with all good things, be careful not to over do. It is not necessary to beat or describe an action for every speech. A simple attributive will often do—and sometimes we don't even need that. The reason to use anything at all is to make it clear to the reader who is speaking. If that's already clear, attributing the speech is unnecessary.

Something to Think About

- Words are not the only way we talk.

- Actions and reactions: Just as with other action/reaction (or stimulus/response) relationships, what one character says drives the second character to respond. Your second character's options are action, more dialogue, exposition, thought (if it is the point-of-view character).

- Beware of dialect. It's hard to do and is often racially or ethnically insensitive. Instead, try to establish it through vocabulary and description of the speech patterns.

- Strike a reasonable balance between action, dialogue, and description. Try to limit it to 10-15% dialogue. The story shouldn't feel like a play.

- If you're trying to be flashy with your language, try bringing it to bear in the beats and in the descriptions of action:

> He stabbed the air in front of Jack's face with his stubby finger. "Listen, Mister," he said. . .

Dialogue Content

Dialogue is never just talk.

Everybody Has an Agenda

Your characters are not stick figures mouthing whatever words you put into their heads. They are real human beings with full lives and internal agendas. In any conversation, each of the speakers carries a significant past. As a result, each has a motive and an attitude—even the most tertiary character, and even on the most casual level.

If your protagonist is ordering coffee in a diner while he waits nervously for the big final scene to unfold, the incidental waitress who takes his order and serves him his drink does so with emotional baggage. Does she hate her job, love to be around people, want a big tip? Is she sad that she's never climbed any higher in life? Is she content? Depressed? Distracted? Abused at home? Worried about her daughter? Anticipating an anniversary celebration? As minor as she is as a character, she is still emotionally invested in her own life. She wants something. When she speaks, everything she says is shaped by her agenda.

Such dynamics are even more true and more crucial for your primary and secondary characters. The waitress may just want your protagonist to drink up and leave, but the conflicting agendas of your major players are vital to the central conflict of the story. While they talk, they all have something they want, and they position themselves and frame their words in order to get it. Some of them state their goals outright. Some are more oblique or even silent on the subject. The point-of-view character may reveal what he wants only through his internal dialogue. But whether the motivation is up front or hidden, its force must be felt by the reader.

In fiction, people never just talk. They argue, they seduce, they wheedle, they plead, they rage. They plot and maneuver. But they don't just talk.

Why Are These People Talking?

While real people often speak just to fill the silence or to kill time or to hear the sound of their own voices, there is no equivalent luxury in story dialogue. Your fictional people must talk with a purpose, always. Space is at a premium, and you have to fill it efficiently, with judicious dialogue choices. That is, you can't put in all the things your characters might say if they were real. Instead, you have to pick only the heightened moments, when your dialogue has a purpose beyond just talk.

As it is for every other element of fiction, the first responsibility of dialogue is to advance the story. Thus, the conversations you include should either build or illustrate the conflict, whether it be the global conflict of the whole story, a momentary conflict between the characters, or the characters united against a common external foe. Even in comedy, there should be some sort of tension, and the talk should have an emotional charge, usually, though not always, as a result of opposing goals among the characters.

In order to advance the story, the dialogue tension should produce a change in the character or the situation. That is, the character feels better or worse, moves closer to or farther from his goal. The relationship between the speakers is deepened or made more estranged. If the net effect is neither gain nor loss, but a static, flatline movement, perhaps you should reconsider including the scene. Ask yourself what good it does the story.

An equally important purpose of dialogue is to reveal character. We judge people by what they say and how they say it as much as by what they do and look like. The content of the speech and the tone with which it is said clearly illustrate the character's thinking. Are his remarks combative, argumentative, kind, evil, snide? His mood, tone, and message all combine to tell us who he is and how we should feel about him.

The level of vocabulary, the chosen syntax, and the manner of speech also provide clues to the kind of person the speaker is. The person who says, "They don't live here no more" is very different from the one who says, "The Pattisons no longer reside at this address"—not only in education and socioeconomic status, but in personality as well. Visualize your characters fully, and they will speak in their own voices.

The best dialogue does all these things. If it doesn't do at least one on a meaningful level, summarize it. Don't have your characters talk just because real people would talk in the scene situation. If the dialogue doesn't make a significant contribution, dump it and find some better moment to quote.

Planting Evidence

Given a choice of medium between exposition and dialogue for revealing information, particularly background, choose exposition. Dialogue revelations often have an awkward, stagey feel about them.

"John, remember when you lost your leg?" Jeff said.

First of all, it's difficult to imagine a circumstance under which one person might really ask another such a question. Second, what are the odds the person addressed would ever forget such an event? More probably, the character is only speaking because the author feels the background information is crucial and has simply picked a poor place to put it. Exposition or narration would be a far better mode.

> In 1984, John Harding had lost his left leg in a hunting accident. He had been bitter about it ever since.

Description, too, can be a problem in dialogue, unless the speaker would naturally be describing what he has seen. If the other characters can see it at the same time or are aware of the details, use straight description instead. The guideline is that you should not state outright what the characters already know and would not say aloud were they real people having a real conversation. When a woman is talking to her husband about their child, she would probably not refer to "our redheaded son, Jimmy," since they both know who Jimmy is and what color hair he has.

The problem comes, then, when you're trying to include information both characters know but the reader doesn't.

> "Sure, I know the guy you mean. They sent him up to Mac, the state reformatory, last fall."

In real speech, it would be unnecessary to include the parenthetical explanation, since both speaker and listener would be likely to know what Mac is. So how do you explain it to the reader in a way that doesn't seem contrived? Use point-of-view narration/exposition. The POV can simply tell us, in this case processing the information to provide perspective as well:

> "Sure, I know the guy you mean. They sent him up to Mac last fall."
> Mac was short for MacNeery, the state reformatory. If Bobby Falwell was there by fourteen, it was probably already too late.

Or you could blend it more subtly into the conversation:

> "Sure, I know the guy you mean. They sent him up last fall."
> "Prison?"
> "Nah. MacNeery. The reformatory. The little punk got off lucky, if you ask me."

One of the writer's most difficult tasks is to provide important background, whether it's technical or descriptive, without it seeming concocted and artificially injected. If you're going to choose dialogue as the mode, you must take special pains that it be a natural part of the conversation. Otherwise, use your point of view to process what we need.

Something to Think About

- Characters speak to each other. Not to us. They speak with one another in mind, and react to what is said *to* them. If you wonder what to say next, look back at what the previous character said.

- By the same token, they wouldn't say what they already know simply because the reader doesn't know it.

- In early drafts, shut off the editor's voice. Allow your characters to babble, without regard to content or editing. You can always cut later—and you *must* cut. But at first their talk can give direction, suggestions of plot and conflict, motivations, characterization, tones, attitudes.

- Characters should be wittier than you are. You have to wait until later, after the moment has passed, to think up snappy comebacks. They can riposte immediately, because they have benefit of your lengthy and thoughtful consideration. There is a distinct difference between writer time and reader time. It may take you a week to come up with something clever for the character to say, but to the reader the remark seems instantaneous.

EXERCISES

6-1. **Dialogue Punctuation:** Paragraph and punctuate the following dialogue.

Richard looked up at his wife as he climbed from the hole   it's no use he said it won't budge   it's got to   put your shoulder into it I've tried that   his face was streaked with sweat   he wiped his mouth with the back of his hand   well she said how about using the shovel darling   you know like a lever or something didn't you hear me he said I told you it won't budge that's okay baby she smiled you done your best

6-2. **Beats:** Pick one of the situations below and list twenty things you might call on for color while the people are talking. Make at least two of them ongoing events which you could use to indicate the passage of time.

  a. A couple are having breakfast at a table in their kitchen while planning where to go for their long-awaited vacation this year.

  b. A couple are arguing about politics while driving along a country road.

  c. A couple are discussing their grown children while they shop for groceries at a large supermarket.

Note that such beats also reflect the character and the conflict. In the first example, for instance, *how* the man butters his toast can indicate the mood of the situation and the character's emotional state as well as his personality type. If he flings the butter on, he is a far different person from one who dabs it on, or one who gouges the bread. How the characters react will be a strong indication of their relationship and the potential for conflict.

6-3. **Visual Clues:** Watch a conversation from a place far enough away to make hearing the words or knowing the content impossible. From your observations, list the visual clues each person gives to his or her mental state. Try for at least twenty.

6-4. **Son of Visual Clues:** A couple are discussing buying something expensive, such as a car. One of them really wants to make the purchase. The other, for whatever reason, does not want to. Write a one-page dialogue in which they discuss the purchase. The objecting partner is forbidden to say so. Use both speech and physical detail to illustrate the tension.

CHAPTER 7

Point of View

When people use the term **narration,** they are referring to explanations of details and events as seen from the **narrator's** perspective, felt the way she would feel and spoken in the language she would use. Simply defined, the point of view (POV) is the narrator's voice. And what the narrator has to say to us can be generally divided into three categories.

First, a great deal of the information in any story will seem purely objective, things which the character sees or hears and then reports to us. Even though such details may seem unattached to a POV, as though a camera were simply recording them, they are actually the narrator's observations. Early in the story, the viewpoint character is set; and from that point on, she is our eyes and ears. And *her* senses are our only source of information:

> Bobby saw the black Chev coming up fast in his rearview mirror.
> An old man slumped in the corner booth, working a fork into the grime under his cracked thumbnail.
> The child shrieked, a long, high-pitched wail sharp enough to etch glass.

The first example above could just as easily be put, "The black Chev was coming up fast in his rearview mirror." If Bobby is our established point of view, all details come to us through him, so it is obvious that the observation is his. As a result, it is usually unnecessary to state outright that he saw or heard something. Note, too, the sense of the narrator's attitude in the second and third examples.

Another kind of observation will be closer to the narrator, presented through touch, smell, and taste—the senses that require contact:

> The air smelled deep-fat-fried.
>
> Michael's heart jumped at the heat of her hand.
>
> The root was dry and bitter.

We could not observe these things from the outside. To whom does the air smell deep-fat-fried? First, it smells that way to the narrator, and through her, it smells that way to us. How do we know what Michael's heart did? Because while the story lasts, we share his nervous system. We feel the stimulus in the form of the warmth from her skin, and then we feel the response in the pitch of his heart.

The third type of observation is closer still. It is the processing done by the narrator—her actual thoughts and feelings about events, people, places—obviously available to us only if we are inside the narrator's head.

> Justin's voice was beginning to grate on my nerves.
>
> She wanted to slap that stupid grin off his face.
>
> Elaine closed her eyes and let the soothing breeze flow over her.

Although the last example may seem like simple description, we can know the breeze is "soothing" only because the narrator tells us. It is the narrator's opinion. That also makes it not the writer's.

Processing

Whenever things happen to us, part of our reaction is physical and part is internal. Between the stimulus and the response, there is always a period during which we process what's going on. How long or short that period is depends upon the circumstances and the kind of people we are. Being told we're going to visit Aunt Sally for the weekend doesn't require immediate reaction, while feeling our footing give way on a clifftop might. On the other hand, Aunt Sally might be a threat of some kind, and news of the visit might give instant rise to such fear that we run screaming from the room.

In fiction, the processing a character does is a function of point of view. That means, we don't get to see any of the actual processing for characters other than the narrator. We may get signs that they are thinking things over—a pensive squint or a bitten lip, for instance—but for the most part, what we see is only the reaction.

For the POV character, however, it truly has to be a different story. Her processing gives us context. When she first hears about the impending visit to Aunt Sally's, for example, she can remember that awful incident in the garden. Through point of view, she can tell us what the problem is—in brief or in detail. It's your call, but if she screams and runs without telling us anything, all we're going to be is mystified.

The character's processing is our entry to her world. Through selected details, language choices, and shared emotional reaction, the narrator tells us how the coffee tastes and how we should feel about the man who just walked through the door. We see the physical world, every detail of it, the way she sees it. As a result, we understand its meanings to her and its impact on her life and on the story. The simple fact of point of view is this: Without *her* perceptions, it is almost impossible for us to have any of our own. Processing lets us in.

The Points of View

One Head at a Time

Before we take on specific points of view, something needs to be said. In real life, we can see through only our own set of eyes. In fiction, life is lived the same way, from only one point of view. As unfair and limiting as that may seem, maintaining a consistent point of view is the one compulsory rule in writing stories. Unfortunately, it is also the one rule with which beginning writers seem to have the hardest time. Probably because examples are everywhere of writers who have broken the rule and gotten away with it. Or because it is so tempting to use what we know. As writers, if we know what's going on in the minds of our other characters (and we should), why can't we just say it? Why should we be so artificially confined to a single point of view?

The main reason is that in fiction, we're trying to imitate reality—even if it's speculative reality. We're trying to capture the sense of one person's life as it is actually lived while the events of the story are taking place. So, unless we're telepathic, that means one head at a time.

Another reason is that we're trying to create a solid, empathetic relationship between the reader and the point-of-view character, one in which the reader feels as though he is simultaneously experiencing what the narrator is going through. If we suddenly shift the point of view, we bump the reader out of the narrator's head—and miraculously into someone else's. No matter how informative that might be in a story, imagine how disconcerting it would be in real life.

The artificiality isn't from being confined to a single point of view. That's the natural part. It's the shifting that's artificial.

The term **omniscience** comes from the Latin *omni,* meaning "all," and *science,* meaning "knowledge." Thus, a truly omniscient narrator is one who is all-knowing, all-seeing, all-wise. The story voice not only knows what is in the head of every character, but all the events—past, present, *and* future—in every location. How real is that? Telepathy aside, most of us cannot actually know the future or hear the thoughts of all the people in a room; we cannot know what goes on in their secret hearts.

If the narrator is to be trusted, you have to maintain a consistent point of view. You can't switch heads just because another character knows something important or because you want to add some interest. You can't become unstuck in time or space with lines like, "Little did he know but at that very moment across town . . ." or "Later, she would be sorry that. . . ." You can't tell us that the heroine will regret her actions *later* when she doesn't know that *now.* And until the point-of-view character discovers him, you can't tell us about a bad guy who's hiding behind a bush around the next bend in the trail.

To keep it real, from the moment the viewpoint character steps onstage, our perceptions are limited to what the narrator knows at the time of the present scene. So, it is wise from the start to pick the POV best able to see the story as it unfolds. In most stories, that's the protagonist.

Among readers, editors, and writers, the two most widely accepted points of view are, in order of preference, **third-person limited omniscience** and **first-person major.**

Third-Person Limited

Person means the person of the pronoun that would refer to the narrator, in this case, third person, *he* or *she:* "He walked into the room" or "Alison McCarty felt a knot of anxiety in her throat."

Third-person limited omniscience is the most popular, and probably the most marketable, point-of-view choice among commercial writers, particularly for longer works. In it, the writer confines observations to the senses and thoughts of a single character. The reader is an eyewitness sitting on or watching over the narrator's shoulder, partner to that one character's life, both external and internal, and no other.

> Jaffrey pinched the pockmarked strip of skin across the bridge of his long, thin nose and waited patiently for Mirabella to get tired of yelling. She had been going at him for half an hour, and now the tiny speck of dark pain that had started when he got up that morning was a ball of white light behind his left eye. Right now, he was only sure of one thing. If she didn't shut up soon, he was going to pass out.

The first sentence of the example signals the POV when it announces what Jaffrey is waiting for, something we assume only he knows. The second sentence confirms the narrator by revealing a physical sensation that cannot possibly be observed by anyone else from the outside. The third sentence presents a general statement about his thinking. The fourth, too, is a POV sentence. While it appears to be an overview statement from the author, its source is actually Jaffrey—his thought, not quoted, but phrased indirectly and summarized. Quoted in direct form, its source is more clear: "If she doesn't shut up soon," he thought, "I'm going to pass out."

In general, the indirect form used in the original is preferred.

Again, note that once the narrator is set for the scene, we cannot change. We cannot switch abruptly to Mirabella to find out why she is yelling at Jaffrey or how she feels about him fiddling with his nose instead of paying attention to her.

If that information is important, there are other ways into your side characters' heads. In real life, for instance, how do you know when someone else is angry with you, or disgusted, or feeling defeated? You know it from the person's body language, from what she says and does. In this case, Mirabella can glare at Jaffrey, or purse her lips, or bare her teeth, or fold her arms across her chest and stomp out of the room. Or she could tell him outright that she's going to knock him silly if he doesn't stop it.

The point is, you must convey such inside information through outside clues which the POV can observe.

On the other end of the spectrum, there is a little breathing room, however. While it is not acceptable to slip into the heads of other characters, it is somewhat more forgivable to slip outside the narrator's head. That is, while comments about the world come from the narrator's point of view, comments about the narrator herself often take the form of *detached narration*:

> Farren Wight was a large man, handsome by most standards, and he carried himself well. He stood in the narrow stone archway,

> balanced uneasily on the balls of his feet, anxiously watching
> Zenna pick over the baubles he had brought to her. She seized a
> ruby the size of an egg between two of her gnarled fingers and
> leered at him over the top of it.

Here, the second sentence clearly establishes Farren Wight as the point of view, since we get to feel the uneasiness of his stance and are privy to his state of mind. The third sentence is also Farren's perception since the choice of language is part of his processing.

But who's saying that first sentence? Whose opinions are those?

Although it is a little more baldly judgmental, it's the same type of information as contained in Jaffrey's description above. It's not really the viewpoint character's observations, and not really the author's either, but a sort of uneasy alliance between the two. Uneasy, because it's "telling;" and so it strains, even if briefly, the reader's tolerance of author intrusion. The strain is not intolerable, but keep such editorial passages brief.

Detached narration also works well in expository openings, where the commentary is about the circumstances presented *before* the narrator has been established. Once it's clear who the point of view is, the exposition becomes narration, processed through the POV.

> Harper was one of those places where people kept their
> heads down. Whatever was going on next door was none
> of their business. It was safer that way, and as long as
> everybody knew the rules, everybody got along. That suited
> Halsey Barnett just fine.

As always, however, even the exceptions have exceptions. In this case, the exception is that detached narration works only in third person. In a first-person story, it can't be "detached," since everything in the story is assumed to come from the first-person narrator, even if we haven't met her yet. For example, if the passage above continues in first person instead of third ("I first met Barnett at a seedy cafe in Old Town"), we would assume that we'd been reading the "I" character's opinions from the start.

The down side to this is that it makes characterization of the narrator a little more difficult in first person. For example, while a first-person Jaffrey might discuss the town of Harper exactly the same way a third-person Jaffrey would, it's a good bet he wouldn't make exactly the same observations about himself. "I pinched the pockmarked strip of skin across the bridge of my long, thin nose . . ." seems oddly inappropriate for self-description, for example. And Farren Wight couldn't tell us he was big and handsome and had good posture without seeming far too egotistical. The net effect is that first-person narrators are often less physically realized than third.

One last pitch for consistency: As mentioned earlier, the chief problem beginning writers have with third-person limited omniscience is staying true to the point of view. There are so many heads in town, it's hard to resist poking around in a few others. The rule on multiple narrators, however, is that within any given scene, you are allowed to be in only one head at a time. Period. The safest course is to tell yourself this:

**In a novel you can change narrators only when you change
scenes or chapters. In a short story, you can't do it at all.**

That said, in a novel, one huge benefit of third-person limited is the increased flexibility. With first person, you're confined solely to the narrator's experience. Anything that takes place out of her presence or beyond her knowledge is unavailable for use in the story unless another character tells her about it. In third-person limited, however, you're confined to only one narrator at a time. At a scene or chapter break, it's perfectly acceptable to switch point of view to another character and present details of which your protagonist is completely ignorant. For instance, a novel whose main character is a police investigator might also have chapters from the criminal's or the victim's POV. As a result, you can more fully develop some of your secondary characters, even your antagonist, although your protagonist should narrate the clear majority of chapters.

First-Person Major

In first person, the narrator is the "I" character. The sense is that the story is less *about* the character than it is *by* him. That is, it feels as though the character is actually telling the story: "I switched on the lamp and stared hard into her eyes"; "The pitch went wild and clipped my chin"; "I felt sick."

While more limited in its scope, first person has its own benefits, primary among which is that the reader gets closer to the point-of-view character. We may still be limited to a single narrator, but we get to know that person very well, especially if she is completely honest with us about what she encounters and how she feels. The personal effect comes from the reader's illusion of being in direct contact with the narrator, without the author as a buffer. In fact, first person often feels to readers as though there is no author at all, only the character sharing all the intimate details and internal processing of what happened.

I looked into his flat black eyes and felt that same bitter bile rise to the back of my throat.

> Mauber's last punch caught me just below the ear and bright lights went off in my head.
>
> Far out over the surface of the pond, a pair of tattered geese rose into the air.

I know, I know. The last example isn't first person at all. In fact, it's third, like most of your sentences will be with a first-person POV. That's because a frequent complaint among people who try first person is what seems to be excessive repetition of the word *I*. One way to avoid the problem is to place the details the narrator observes in third person instead and omit the first-person references entirely. Rather than say, "I watched the lush landscape rush by outside my train window," say, "The lush landscape rushed by the train window." Since *all* the observations in first person come from the narrator, it isn't necessary to include "I saw" or "I heard." Readers will know the narrator perceived it.

Many writers find first person easier to write. They simply put on the "I" mask and "become" the protagonist, seeing as she sees, thinking as she thinks. The danger is that while it is easier for you to identify with your primary, it is also easier for you to blur the line between creator and persona. You becoming your character can be very beneficial. Your character becoming you is not. For aesthetic distance (and for sanity), you want to create a narrator with her own sense of being.

Another benefit is that first person also keeps point of view consistent. With third person you may tend to wander into any third-person head; but with first, because the narrator is always "I," you always know which head you are supposed to be in. The drawback is that regardless of whether the mode is scene or exposition, the narrator must always be present. She must always be the voice.

Since there is no detached narration in first person, all the nondialogue commentary about the events of the story comes only from her. The ultimate effect is that first person feels more intimate to readers. Because the story is, in essence, one long confession, we get to meet the narrator on a more personal level than we would with third person. The two cautions are (1) that your narrator must be someone worth listening to, and (2) that your reader shouldn't have to listen to too much. You can't let your POV get on a soapbox or wax poetic about every little thing. First person or third, readers are here for the story, not for a lecture.

Another sticking point is that physically, first-person narrators are often not very well drawn. While the internals of the narrator may be easier in first person, the externals are more difficult. Remember, in first person, all observations come from the narrator. That means that while some disembodied voice is talking about the narrator in detached third-person narration, in first person she is talking about herself. How much time should you spend on that? What kinds of comments are appropriate for her to make?

For instance, would your character ever state, "A tremor ran down my chiseled face"? Doubtful. It simply sounds too egotistical. Where detached narration works just fine in third person, such testimonials (even if they are unflattering) sound phoney or inappropriate. Even the more subtle method of giving longer, more detailed descriptions of the character and letting readers reach their own conclusions doesn't work well. Why would anyone go on that way about himself? It simply sounds too forced for the character to stop and tell us about herself, and a reflection in a mirror or store window is a terrible cliché. So what are you supposed to do if you want to give a clear physical picture of your first-person POV?

For one thing, you must limit the space you take up with description. No long blocks like the ones you might find in detached narration. Instead, present smaller pieces of the character as you move through the story. On page 1, she might adjust her glasses to read a menu, for example, or push a wisp of hair off her face and complain briefly about its color or texture. Or she might find a hair on her husband's shirt and compare it to her own. In other words, use your narrator's actions and reactions within the circumstances to convey physical detail. Try to have the description triggered by some other element of the story.

Can I Get a Witness? First-Person Minor

In most stories that you write, the first-person narrator is going to be the major character, the protagonist. An interesting twist on that is the *first-person minor* narrator, someone who is not such an active participant in the major conflict, but more of an observer, a witness to a story that happens to someone else.

This POV allows you to get some of the intimacy associated with a first-person major narrator. Remember, however, the first-person minor is not the main player in the story and thus doesn't need too much intimacy. In addition, you might also get some of the benefits of detached narration, since the narrator can generally comment more freely on the protagonist than the protagonist can comment on herself.

The problems with first-person minor seem to outweigh the advantages, however. For one thing, it removes readers one step further from identification with the major character and may cause them to identify more with the minor narrator. If readers like to "become" the character, which one should they choose if given a choice? Probably not a minor player.

Another problem is simply logistical: What do you do if something really important happens to the main character and the narrator isn't there to see it?

I don't know if Daddy fought with her like that when they went out, but sometimes the front door would slam at three or four in the morning, and I would hear his heavy footsteps pacing the kitchen floor until I fell back asleep.

In other words, the first-person minor can only provide clues, can guess and speculate about what goes on off camera. That sometimes leaves the reader guessing as well—which has both benefits and detriments.

A Word on Second Person

Where third person tells readers *about* the character and the first-person narrator talks *to* the reader, second person demands that the reader *be* the character. "You sit in the hard, cold chair and fidget, listening to formless echoes in the hallway, gnawing a fingernail until they call your name."; "The bullet grazes your temple and darkness explodes in your head."

In general, readers hate being ordered around that way. You write,"You walk into the room." The reader balks; and the moment he says, "No, I don't, and you can't make me," you've lost him.

The word on second person? *Don't.*

Keeping Your Distance

While the two most acceptable points of view fall somewhere in the middle of the spectrum, there are extremes as well, based on how close the writer gets to the narration.

For example, when fiction was relatively young, detached narration wasn't so detached. Authors often took a very active role in the story, stepping in at will to comment liberally on characters and events. Such *author presence* not only told readers what was happening and who was there, but how to feel as well: "Recoil, dear reader! The horror she faces will be more than she can bear." Apologies to literary scholars, but it is doubtful that such writers could get published today. Contemporary audiences (and thus, editors) much prefer to let the story physically unfold as it will, without comment from anyone but the narrator.

At the other end of the scale is the *dramatic* or *external* point of view, which presents the story through physical descriptions only. Actions and dialogues are presented objectively, in language as free from slant as possible and without internal processing. While the author is not present in the story, neither is the narrator. The events are reported solely from the outside and we are never in anyone's head. The difficulties with external POV are twofold: First, since nearly all our descriptive words are emotionally loaded in some way, complete objectivity is nearly impossible. Second, if one of the reasons readers read in the first place is to identify with the character, such a specifically limited POV seems to be grossly counterproductive.

Something to Think About

- "Processing, the Sequel": We can often tell what kind of person the narrator is by the content, depth, and type of her thoughts.

- The amount of processing can also have an effect on the pace of the story. Obviously, a high-action tale with only brief processing moves much more quickly than a philosophical story.

- Using an involved narrator enhances the conflict, since we can see the cause-and-effect nature of the character's internal struggles—what hurts her, troubles her, gladdens her, and why.

- The type and amount of processing should be appropriate to the physical circumstances. A soldier being shot at, for instance, probably wouldn't pause too long to think before she ducked. Maybe she wouldn't think at all.

- In a novel, third-person limited omniscience increases the potential for suspense. Just as the POV character is about to reach a moment of crisis or discovery, cut to another character.

- Just as you should avoid the use of "I saw" in first person, you can do the same with "he saw" in third by simply describing what was seen. "Beauchamp saw the dark man raise his gun" becomes "The dark man raised his gun," which feels a little more as if we're seeing it ourselves rather than being told about it. Whenever possible, avoid constructions like "he saw," "I felt," "she heard."

- Beware the character who is simply a mouthpiece, one who is only a front for the author.

- In first-person stories, all the elements are filtered through the narrator's personality and are thus colored by her emotional view of the world. Consider a story in which the narrator is self-serving, bigoted, a liar.

- In first person, some tension is taken away, since the reader knows the narrator will not die.

EXERCISES

7–1. **Internals:** Consult what you wrote in response to Exercise 2–1, in which you listed ten to thirty purely physical things a young man might notice as he climbs a bridge in order to jump into the river below. Remember that one of his friends has egged him on, that it's a warm day, and that there are people sunbathing by the water.

For the next five minutes, speedlist the things he might *think* as he climbs. Again, try for at least ten. And again, twenty to thirty would even be better.

7–2. **Externals:** Write a one-page scene in which two people are arguing over something important to both of them. Confine yourself to only one of their points of view. Underline all the things you have done to show how the other person feels—dialogue, physical description, suppositions by the narrator, for example.

7–3. **Processing:** A man has been dating a woman for about six months. He loves her and plans to ask her to marry him after their theater date tonight. Suddenly, he remembers leaving the tickets on his kitchen table. It's too late to go back and get them. He confesses, thinking that maybe a quiet evening at home is a better setting anyway. But the woman begins to berate him for his carelessness, his stupidity not just this evening, but over the course of their relationship. She slaps him.

In the next five minutes, list ten things he might think. Note that his thoughts both process the input and decide on an appropriate reaction.

Reverse the roles and repeat the exercise. Compare the two lists of thoughts for consistency as well as differences. To what are the differences accountable?

CHAPTER 8

Style

Only after considerable practice should you begin to worry about style. At the start, you should be much more concerned about creating whole, believable characters and telling a good story. In fact, style is probably more a reflection than a creation. That is, the style will naturally follow from the story and the author. Your ear will know what sentence length or language level is appropriate for a given passage, as well as how much time and development to give it. Yet, as you continue to write, fine-tuning stylistic considerations will become more important to you, and you will learn to play with the variables in your head as a matter of habit.

Mode

Much as a painter has a choice of types of paint, various tools for applying it, and a broad assortment of surfaces, so does the fiction writer have a choice of media with which to work. Indeed, much of what we call an author's style depends on the pace of the story, and that's a function of mode. Some writers are famous for giving their readers high-action sequences that zip by at a breakneck pace, with clipped dialogue, and terse descriptions. Others take a more leisurely, contemplative stance and allow their narrators to process each action and observation at great length before the next takes place.

Given any single piece of information, we are faced with a wealth of ways to present it. The choice affects the rate at which information is taken in and the rate at which the story seems to move.

While there are pieces in which the authors have tried to use only one mode, usually stories are a combination. Deciding which ones to use when and how much of each at any given time makes mode one of the great stylistic balancing acts of fiction.

Action is the physical movement of the scene. It quickens the pace and causes the reader to get physically involved. Imagine attending a movie with your eyes closed and having a friend describe in vivid detail what is happening on the screen. While it takes longer, action is nearly always preferable to exposition and summary. Having your character do something that shows him as quick-tempered is much stronger than just telling us. It isn't necessary, however, to include every small movement. And too much action stays too much on the surface of things. Even action can seem too report-like without any internalizations.

Dialogue is the vocal equivalent of action. This also moves the story very quickly, unless, of course, the speaker is long-winded or preachy, or if you use a character as your own ventriloquist's dummy. It also breaks up the page by yielding more white space, which readers can find less intimidating and easier to read. As a consequence, editors love it. Dialogue allows characters to share information and establishes each character's style as well. If it is overused, however, the story becomes a play, or worse, just talking heads. In general, dialogue should be no more than 10 or 15 percent of the whole.

Thoughts are closely related to dialogue, but they're one-sided and often presented in larger blocks than a speech would be. Since the character reveals his thoughts, the reader is provided direct access and insight, which makes the character's reactions both reasonable and real. The more cerebral the narrator, however, the slower the story. Overuse of thought can be boring and too personal, unless the character is interesting enough to carry it off. If the character isn't, he'll come off as tedious. The extreme form of thought is **stream of consciousness,** thoughts as they might actually occur in the head—a central theme while tangential pictures and ideas flare up and trail off at random. Stream of consciousness should probably be used only as a device, not as a worklong mode.

Summary moves the story at its fastest pace. These are the generalizations we use to compress time and impressions into a short space. Life is made up of far too many details to capture entirely accurately on the page. Sixty pages wouldn't be enough to show everything that happens in a five-minute span. Six hundred still might not be enough. So you're forced to hit only the highlights. The stylistic compromise is the level at which you decide to generalize, how many details you're willing to leave out and for what purpose. Summary works well to move time, for instance, since you leave out all the dull things that happen in real life and get to the active parts of the story. But summaries of people, places, and events scrimp on development and are not quite so effective. They should be replaced or supplemented by description or action which captures the essence. Not *silly man*, for instance, but a quick image or action that shows the character.

Description gives the feel of physical immediacy. We all relate better to those things we perceive with our senses, so the idea is to get your readers' senses to engage. Details they can visualize or smell or taste will draw them physically into the story and make them feel as though they are actually living it. As a tool, description is used for anything from static landscape to the lively pictures of the characters' actions. Try to use vivid language and sensory descriptions. *Bolted* and *raced*, instead of *ran*, for example, or *old woman with a lined face* instead of simply the more anonymous summary *old woman*. Overuse of description, however, leads to a work which is tedious or pointless, filled with long passages of detail that have no impact on the story. Description is a tool, not an end.

Exposition and **narration** are the "telling" parts of the story, the explanations, the reflections on the situations. They are, in effect, a narrative equivalent of summary. After a story element, such as a person or a setting, is introduced, the prose steps back to explain what the element is and why it is important. The distinction between the two terms is that exposition is from a detached source, while narration is from the character's point of view. In general, after the POV is established, the explanations should give a sense that they are the narrator's observations. Such passages can actively clarify the situation, since the reader gets not only the physical details, but how they affect the narrator. Overuse of exposition or narration slows the story considerably, actually bringing the forward momentum of the plot to a stop while an essay takes place.

Dealing with the Past

Characters do not come to us outside time. They have pasts, lives they led before the opening line of the story. Most of the past, like most of real life, is too dull to warrant a whole story, but every character will have incidents important enough to affect how he is to act in the story in front of us—a traumatic childhood event that makes the character afraid of heights, for instance, or the loss of a loved one which makes her unready to face the world. The puzzle is how to weave those incidents into the prose in a manner that adds to the plot rather than distracting from it.

Dialogue is probably the least intrusive method of presenting back-story, since it is a natural part of the flow of the scene. One character simply explains something another needs to know about the past. (*Note:* If both characters already know, there is usually little point to them talking about it. As a result, it can seem too obvious that you are manipulating a conversation the characters probably wouldn't have under normal circumstances. You'll need to take special pains to keep the dialogue from seeming contrived.)

Memory is another excellent means of revealing the point-of-view character's past. An event or an object triggers the character into thinking about the past. The stimulus is clear and the memory is a reasonable response. Because it interrupts the story, keep it quick and germane.

Exposition and narration are the *telling* of the story. They are longer than memory and consist of an essay about the significant past. A character walks into the scene, and the narrator (or author) uses the opportunity to pause and tell us the background information. If you choose this means, it's usually better to present the explanation stretched across the current scene, to break up the information with pieces of an ongoing action, for example.

Flashback, unlike memory, is longer and interrupts the current action with an actual scene from the character's past. The purpose is to enhance the present story by clearly illustrating an incident in the past. Flashback should be an addition to the story, not the main story itself.

Diction

Language and word choice go a long way toward establishing the story's tone of voice, which should be appropriate to the content of the piece.

Language Level

Edited: Somewhat formal, nonthreatening; the most prevalent choice among fiction and nonfiction writers alike. It gives the illusion of conversation, but doesn't have the looseness of colloquial English.

Formal: Scholarly and pretentious; usually too stiff or stuffy sounding to be of much use anywhere other than the dialogue of a stiff or stuffy person.

Colloquial: Conversational, casual; may be a bit too informal to carry most fiction unless the story is told from the mouth of the persona, as though the character were speaking it.

Regional: Captures speech of a limited geography. As with colloquial English, it may be too informal (or too distracting) for most fiction, although it works well in local color pieces.

Nonstandard: Dialect, slang, "substandard" English; difficult to maintain, sometimes insulting in its tone and inept translations from spoken to written form.

Sound

Often, if you watch people in the act of reading, you will see their lips move. That's because most of us read with a subvocal voice. We sound the words out in our heads. It would be wise, therefore, to develop the practice of reading your work aloud to feel how it strikes the ear. Elements of rhythm, lilt, and word sounds then come into play on a level you might never have suspected exists in the writer's craft. English words that find their origins in Anglo-Saxon, for instance, are often short, abrupt, rough-sounding. Conversely, Latin- and Greek-based words can be longer, smoother, more elegant-sounding: *eviscerate* instead of *gut*, or *perspire* instead of *sweat*.

As nitpicky as these distinctions may sound, eventually you'll want to choose the right words for each passage, each action, each sentence.

Syntax (Sentence Structures)

Simple: A simple subject with a simple verb and usually a simple predicate: *Shelly slipped quietly to the floor. Roger grabbed the phone.*

Used for action sequences and for emphasizing detail, the simple sentence has a staccato effect that can seem unsophisticated if it's overused. It can also provide relief from some of the more ponderous styles.

Compound Predicate: The sentence is still simple in its construction: *Roger grabbed the phone and punched the buttons furiously.*

Used to avoid a Dick-and-Jane style and to combine information.

Compound: Combines subjects and actions with two or more main clauses in a single sentence: *Shelly slipped quietly to the floor, and Roger grabbed the phone.*

Clearly establishes relationships among the subjects and their actions. Also improves the flow of information, since the reader doesn't have to stop at sentence ends as frequently. Note the sense of sequence.

Complex: The use of phrases and dependent clauses in conjunction with the main part of the sentence: *As Shelly slipped quietly to the floor, Roger grabbed the phone.* Or *Shelly slipped quietly to the floor before Roger grabbed the phone.*

Allows the reader to concentrate on the main idea of the sentence while still perceiving satellite information. Also improves flow.

Compound-Complex: Two or more main ideas, *plus* one or more dependent clauses: *As Shelly slipped quietly to the floor, Roger reached for the phone and the dog began to howl.*

You should try to vary your sentences as you write. Too many simple sentences give your writing a primary-school feel. Too many complex or compound-complex sentences make the story ponderous.

Emphasis

What goes where? And in which order? Which information is most important? Usually, the ending of the sentence has more weight than the beginning.

Cumulative: *Jerry gave in to the temptation, once he understood resistance was useless.*

The action comes first, followed by the information.

Periodic: *Once he saw that resistance was useless, Jerry gave in to the temptation.*

Information first, then action.

Parenthetical: *Once he saw that resistance was useless, the sweet smell of chocolate swelling in his nose, Jerry gave in to the temptation.*

Information, then parenthetical explanation, then action.

Symbolism

In real life, the details around us are not dramatically heavy with meaning. They are simply the realities we live in, the physical world that we react to and that reacts to us—unless we contrive to give them meaning. For example, August 25 has no inherent significance until we make it have one—because it is a birthday, or the anniversary of some important event. Otherwise it is just another day. A rose is just another flower. And a flower is just another weed. What makes them mean anything more? We do. We decide.

Symbolism is the act of investing something with a meaning that goes beyond simple physical value. It is not nearly as mystical a process as literary scholars and film critics would have us believe. It is simply the drawing of associations that evoke meaning other than on the literal level. A woman slaps her dog three times. The fourth time she raises her hand, even the dog can see the meaning of the gesture.

We are free to apply symbolism to virtually anything. If a mean-hearted character uses a cigarette holder, the object becomes associated with the attitude. The kind of car we drive, the clothes we wear, the manner of speech, the hair styles, the tattoos—all have meaning beyond the literal. If Billy drives his car from Point A to Point B, there is little symbolic value. If he drives his Porsche, it says something else; if Billy is seventeen and he drives the Porsche his father bought him, a third thing.

Classic symbols associate an object or a name or an action with someone or something else—allusions to Christ, for instance, or to Lady Macbeth. A man uses a section of garden hose to save a child trapped under water. The hose is symbolic of an umbilical cord, the water the fluid of life—and of death. The hose is green because green is the color of life. The child is the rebirth of the man. Yikes! Too much, by a long ways.

At this stage of the game, it's probably better to leave symbolism to the literary masters. Most readers of popular fiction have an inherent distrust of writers who try too hard, who employ gimmicks. They have a right to expect a straight story. Don't depend on their getting your symbols. They're under no obligation to catch what you're trying to say, especially if you're too oblique or too obscure.

If you're driven to symbolize, however, keep it on this level: Everything has symbolic value, even our words. A wife and husband are dressing to go out for the evening. He comes into the living room dressed in a plaid sport-coat she was going to give to charity. She says, "Are you going to wear that?" Aren't there more levels of meaning to what she is asking than simply confirming what her eyes can easily see? Doesn't the coat also symbolize something to her? What are the various things she might also be saying and what meanings may the coat have to them both?

Something to Think About

- Tone is the voice of your prose, the attitude of your vocabulary choices. It's a slippery matter, and one we often deny exists. If you've ever had someone say to you, "It's not what you said, it's the way that you said it," if you've ever argued over such a statement, you know just how slippery it is. At its best, your tone of voice is the emotional quality the work sets. At its worst, it is author intrusion. If there is an attitude, it should always be the character's.

- **Profanity:** If your character is the type, put it in. If he's not, leave it out. It's a sign of a tiny mind, either the character's or the writer's. What do you really think about people who consciously try to manipulate you through shock? Even if you can accept the profanity, you're likely to rebel at the manipulation. More frequently, overuse of profanity marks you as an author with a small vocabulary.

- Do not use unusual words more than once in a chapter or story.

- **Precise language:** Try to find the right verb. Adverbs are okay, but they're really only approximations of what we mean to say. Somewhere out there is the verb we really want. The most effective use of adverbs is to describe physical verbs, not mental states. *Ran quickly* is acceptable, for instance, while *watched sadly* would be better defined by description and action. Let the reader come to the conclusion about the state of mind.

- **Paragraphing:** Generally, the first sentence rules the paragraph. In expository writing, it's called the topic sentence. It focuses the central idea of the information of the coming paragraph and tells the reader exactly what to expect from it. If the topic sentence is "Mark Twain drew brilliant characterizations," the reader has the right to expect only that subject and only that central idea to be discussed in that paragraph. The same rule applies in fiction, if a little more broadly. What you mention in Line 1 should be the major thread of the paragraph. When the focus changes, change paragraphs.

- Avoid *very* and *really*. Under normal circumstances, they don't accomplish anything but make your writing seem amateurish and forced. That is, the emotion or condition is so important that you fear your reader won't get it: "He was a big man" versus "He was a very big man"; "a really steep cliff." If you feel the need to intensify the moment, do it through stronger language choices and descriptions.

- Unnecessary evils:

> I thought to myself . . . [As opposed to thinking it to another person, for instance?]
> When she was alive, my mother used to tell me stories.
> A convulsive cough he could not control
> He repeated himself again.

- Wherever possible, avoid "There was," "There were," and "There are" constructions. Their grammatical subjects are too vague. We need a sense of focus, someone or something engaging in an action.

> There was a tall cabinet against the back wall.
> A tall cabinet stood against the back wall.

A similar problem exists with indefinite pronouns, as in the sentence "It had been hard to finish the speech." To what does *It* refer?

- State-of-being verbs *(is, are, was, were, had been, will be, could be)* have no physical impact. In a very real sense, fiction writing is a visual art. You count on words to trigger pictures in your readers' heads. The more your language choices contain an appeal to the senses, the more the reader will be drawn in.

- Passive voice:

> Debris could be heard falling all around him.
> An eagle was seen.

The fault is not the verb, but the fact that no one is taking a role in the action. Who's hearing the debris? Who's seeing the eagle? Whether the focus of the revision is the perceiver or the object perceived, always make the subject the active element in the sentence.

> He heard debris falling all around.
> Debris crashed around him.
> An eagle dipped low across the surface of the water.

- Try not to bury important information in a sentence or paragraph with another focus. Give the information emphasis of its own.
- Avoid onomatopoeia—the imitation of sound on paper. The attempt is to make it immediate. The effect is comic.

> *"Aaaarrgh!"*   Instead, say, *He screamed.*
> *BANG!   An explosion ripped the room.*
> *Rrrriiing.   The alarm clock rang.*

- Also avoid using exclamation points and putting anything in all capital letters. Allow the prose, not the punctuation or typography, to carry the emotion. It's as if you're trying to argue your readers into the feeling, instead of simply presenting the scene well and allowing them to judge for themselves whether it deserves the emotion.
- Advice on clichés: *Avoid them like the plague.*

At one time, that particular phrase was probably wonderfully rich. That's why it became popular—so popular that it simply slipped into the language and lost its sensory effect. The original writer was trying to evoke a picture so serious it would scare the bejeezus out of people. When he invented the phrase, medicines were ineffective and the plague could kill—and in none too pretty a way. His first readers probably shuddered. Today, however, the simile is so overused it no longer evokes any imagery at all. The plague picture is missing entirely.

EXERCISES

8-1. **Clichés**: Retire the following clichés by inventing new ways of describing what they describe. Try to capture the drama they once may have had. To make ten, add two of your own choosing. Use each in a sentence.

To be fired up	The light at the end of the tunnel
Hard as nails	To break someone's will
Have a short fuse	To nail something
Bird brain	Wired

8-2. **Name that Mode**: Using a passage of no more than 1,000 words from your favorite author, find and transcribe one example of each of the following modes:

Action	Summary
Dialogue	Description
Thought	Exposition/Narration

a) Which mode seems to dominate the passage? Is that true for other sections of the story or book? Is that mode choice typical of the author's style?

b) Within the same passage, how much information is there about the past, i.e., about past events or people? What is the dominant mode for presenting such information (dialogue, memory, exposition, or flashback)?

8-3. **Symbols**: What do each of the following signify to you? Most will mean more than one thing. Quicklist five for each.

a swastika tattoo	long fingernails
a new BMW	Spring
a baby	the dark
a tie	bloodshot eyes
the color blue	an old tree

How universal do you think your interpretations are? Could the objects/concepts be used to symbolize the meanings you perceive for them?

8-4. **Symbols, Part Two:** Write a scene in which a grown person has returned to settle the affairs of a recently deceased parent. The character is in the parent's home, which could be the house where the character grew up or a room in a nursing home. As the character moves through the setting, he/she observes details which evoke both the parent's recent lifestyle and the POV's past.

Appendixes

Research

How do you set a story in Argentina if you've never been to Argentina? How do you make your hero a soldier if you've never had any military experience? How do you ever write any fiction about times other than your own?

Research.

On the upside of research, you will be in a better position to write what you know if you know more things. Often, precise writing is not so much a matter of getting it right, as of not getting it wrong. If you're knowledgeable and comfortable with the subject, you don't have to worry about stuttering over accuracy.

In addition, research can open new avenues to you. As you learn, you'll be inspired. You may find small details that point you toward new plot twists, arcane bits of information that lead to increased possibilities for your characters' actions.

Yet, as much as it has to recommend it, research can also work against a writer. First of all, you must be sure that it is not simply a very attractive stall technique. Many of us will do anything to convince ourselves that we are writing or preparing to write, when in fact we are only stalling. We read voraciously, we delve into every dark recess of the subject, we make copious notes, all to strengthen our prose when the moment comes, but we're not writing.

Another drawback to research is that our writing can easily get bogged down in technical detail. We have invested so much time and have discovered so much fascinating detail, that we feel we have to get it all onto paper. Our readers will be as fascinated as we are, right? Sometimes yes, sometimes no. It depends on your style and your story, but you might ask yourself if you need the extra burden. You might be better off to research *after* you have written the story.

Remember, our first obligation is to tell the story, to keep the reader entertained. Even the most fact-filled historical fiction keeps that rule in mind. Our readers may come away greatly informed, but they are kept reading by the tale itself.

Start Simple

If writing is a business, consider how much time research takes and what it may cost—for example, to buy research books and to travel. Consider what all this does to your hourly wage. You may only wish for accuracy in your art, regardless of the cost, or it may seem like fun because you love learning, but the fact is research is part of the writing process. Keeping that perspective may keep you on task.

Backgrounds

How many different kinds are there? Historical, social, ethnic, cultural, to name a few. Do not content yourself with the simple surface. How would you know the psychology of a Japanese character if all you read was a tourist guide of Japan? "Field studies," such as books about doing business with the Japanese or sociological inquiries, will stand you in much better stead. Look for books that can give you the "character" rather than simply the facts. And in your writing, try to make use of the arcane.

Make a Research Plan

Are you looking for information or inspiration? What do you want to know? Is it important to know that? Who would know it? What sources would care enough to tell you about it?

Sources

Libraries   Wander the library to find out where things are. In libraries organized around the Library of Congress system, books on related fields are near one another. Look at the spines and titles. Learn how to string-search a catalog, whether it is on computer or in hard copy files, so that your range broadens first, then narrows as you need it to. Once you find a helpful book, check the bibliography for more.

Make use of what is probably the most valuable research tool in the library—the librarian.

Does your town have any special-collection libraries?

Special Libraries Association Directory (SLA)—Most large libraries have local directories of libraries for law firms, government agencies. Access is often available only on request.

Guide to Reference Books—Abstracts of books on a variety of subjects.

Reader's Guide to Periodical Literature—Index of magazine articles.

Other periodical guides specific to certain fields are also available.

Book Stores   Your own collection of books saves much travel and research time. At the very least, you should have a fairly large hardbound dictionary, a good paperback dictionary for quick reference, and a thesaurus (organized by concept, *not* alphabetically). Another handy reference is a visual dictionary, which provides pictures of objects and labels their parts and kinds. Types of hats, for instance, or parts of the human hand.

Associations   Professional organizations, such as chambers of commerce, the bar association, and the police, often have their own publications and/or libraries. In addition, they may have a person who is willing to talk to you about your subject.

Government   Your tax dollar at work. There are all sorts of publications and offices out there. Consult your phone book and your librarian.

The Phone Book   A valuable source not only of character names, but of businesses that might be related to your field of interest, government resources, calendars to the year 2025, directories of community service organizations, city maps, and on and on. Even phone numbers.

Personal Contacts and Friends   Ask around, or just listen. What your friends know might start your motor.

Local Societies and Clubs   From stamp collecting to game hunting, from historical societies to hate mongers, the array of local interests is vast and rife with possibilities.

Interviews   If you're not shy, set up interviews with people who have expertise.

Planned Conversations   Where might people be or gather who would know something about your subject? Hang around until you're a familiar face, or strike up a conversation.

Paid Sources   Use "informants" or professional consultants.

The Internet   This resource is seemingly endless and filled with glorious possibilities. You can have instant access to information it might take you weeks to track down otherwise. Be completely aware of the time you spend, however. It's far too easy to lose track as link leads on to link. You know what a staller you are.

A note of caution to those people who need "do not drink" labels on cans of house paint: Use your head. Don't put yourself in jeopardy for the sake of research.

Publication and Market Research Exercise

You know what *you* want to write. But what does the *market* want?

This exercise reverses the usual approach to publication, which is to write a story and then cast desperately about for a place to publish it. Instead, perhaps you should try to find the magazine before you write, and then tailor a story to fit the market. I know this takes some of the romance out of being a writer, but it could prove useful to you, if only as an exercise in craft. Besides, writing as a professional often means writing what sells. A little planning might help your writing to fit a preexisting market. It might not only save you marketing time, but provide inspiration for your writing—which is often hard to come by.

Your magazine profile should consist of at least the following:

1. What is the title? How often is the magazine published? What is the price per edition? Per subscription? How old is the magazine? What is the name of the editor and address for submissions? What other information about submissions is listed on the masthead page?

2. If the magazine is listed in the *Writer's Market,* copy the entire entry. Analyze the entry in terms of what is suitable. Do the editors give any guidance? Write a brief comment on the advice, as well as your feelings about the magazine based on the entry. What is the rate of pay?

3. How many stories are published per issue? What is the length of each? Minimums and maximums? Are there any continuing pieces or excerpts?

4. Audience: Who reads the magazine? Gender, age, socioeconomic status? What interests? Analyze the advertising, if there is any, to get a feel for what the readers think about life.

5. Write a short list of value adjectives characterizing the magazine— your impressions from the articles, cartoons, artwork, features, and so on.

6. What types of stories are unsuitable? What makes you think so?

7. Stories:

   What genre types? (Romance, action, western, science fiction, mystery, etc.)

   How do they begin? (In medias res, with exposition, etc.)

General sentence length?

Language level?

What kinds of endings?

Are the tones upbeat, sad, tragic?

What character types dominate the stories—in both physical and mental traits?

8. Propose and/or roughly outline a type of story which might appeal to the editor and audience, *and* explain why you think so.

9. Money issues: What kind of rights would you be selling? What is the rate of pay? Per word or flat fee? If you were to write the story you have proposed, how long would it take you to finish a publishable draft? Do the math to figure your hourly rate of pay.

Note: You should read (not thumb through or glance at) at least three issues of the magazine in order to get a feel for the typical makeup. You're studying to advance your career.

Manuscript Style

The manuscript you send to a publisher is the rough equivalent of the face you present in a job interview. No matter how clever you may be, no matter how forceful your words or dazzling your ideas, all your brilliance isn't worth a bag full of dryer lint if the only thing on the interviewer's mind is the spinach between your teeth. In other words, first impressions count. In this case, if you want the job, you have to look good.

While standards vary from editor to editor, here are some general guidelines for placing black on white.

First, I know of no editor who accepts handwritten work. Your manuscript should be typed or printed. Start with white paper. It should be standard letter size—8 1/2 by 11 inches. While a good-quality bond with some kind of fiber content gives the manuscript a classy look, you should know that it is perfectly acceptable (not to mention cheaper) to use twenty-pound multiuse paper stock. Under no circumstances, however, should you use either onionskin paper or erasable bond (even if you're typing and your typing is atrocious). Onionskin is simply too thin, although it has the time-saving benefit of allowing the editor to read the entire manuscript without having to turn a single page. As far as erasable bond goes, the same quality that makes it erasable also allows the editor to blot up the print with her thumb and reprint it on every surface she touches. Probably not the way to win friends and influence publishers.

Double-space your lines. For one thing, it seems more reader friendly because it's both easier to read and less intimidating than a solid block of black. In addition, if the editor should approve the manuscript, double spacing leaves room for the editorial comments and proofreading.

The print itself should be letter-quality, whether you type or use a laser or inkjet printer. If you're typing, make sure your ribbon has life left in it. If you're computer-printing, the toner should give clear, crisp print for the whole manuscript. Avoid using dot-matrix printers entirely.

The typeface should be clear, and approximately a twelve-point font, although the twelve-point default font on some word-processing programs is still a little small. In general, you should get about 12 to 14 words to the line and about twenty-four double-spaced lines (250 to 300 words) to the page. If the editor has to squint or is put off even in the slightest by the sense of too many words squeezed together in too small a space, you've lost much of the battle before the editor even gets past the first page. Many will simply return the manuscript unread.

No fancy fonts. No italics. No swirling, swooping nineteenth-century script. And especially, no cute clip art or graphic designs to "help" the story along. Dazzling the editor with empty gimmicks won't sell your manuscript. Just use a plain, workhorse font that places the story in front of the reader without any annoying distractions. Courier, Times New Roman, or Arial, for instance.

If there is a gimmick at all, it should be in the amount of white space. On the page itself, the print should look uncrowded. Use margins of approximately one inch on the bottom and the right, and approximately an inch and a quarter at the top and left. Do not justify the right margin.

Generally, there is no need to include a title page with a short story. The placement of the title and the existence of other pertinent information should be clues enough that the top page of your story is, in fact, the first page. Begin by putting your name, address, and phone number in the upper-left-hand corner. Also, put an approximate word count in the upper left. About one-third to one-half-way down the first page, center the title either in all capital letters or in initial caps. Double-space and center the word *by*, then double-space again and center your name. Double-space twice more and begin the actual story.

Headers and footers: On every page but the first, put your last name, a slash (or colon), and the title (if it's short) in the upper-left-hand corner. If the title is long, put just the first few words—enough so the manuscript can be easily identified. Every page should also be numbered, usually either in the upper-right-hand corner or centered at the bottom of the page.

If the ending of your story comes close to the bottom of the last page, indicate that it is the end by typing—what else?—"The End." If the ending lands earlier on the page, it's probably not necessary to do anything at all.

The overriding rule is this: Keep it clean and neat and readable. While no editor ever bought a story simply because it looked good on the page, most simply refuse even to read a story that looks bad.

Something to Think About

- Always include a self-addressed, stamped envelope, known in the trade as the *SASE*. Not only is the SASE good if you want your manuscript back, but many editors won't even read a story unless the SASE is with it.

- The SASE should have sufficient postage and be of sufficient size to contain the manuscript. Don't use a nice nine-by-twelve-inch manilla envelope to submit the work and expect the editor to jam it all into a Number 10 business envelope with a single stamp for the return. If you do submit with only a Number 10 SASE, don't expect to get the manuscript back, although that size envelope is probably perfect for a boilerplate rejection slip.

- Taking a licking: Try to use an SASE the editor doesn't have to lick to close. And attach the stamps yourself.

- Be patient. A six- to eight-week turnaround for submissions is fairly typical, but it is not unheard of to take four months.

- With the advent of personal printers, this advice applies less now than it used to, but some editors want only originals—no photocopies. When an editor gets a photocopy, she has every right to assume that you've submitted the original elsewhere and her magazine was not your first choice.

- About multiple submissions: Don't do it. If you submit a story to two places at once, what will you do if both magazines accept? Since the act of submitting a manuscript indicates your willingness to have the story published, it's possible, especially in smaller presses, that both magazines would already be in the layout process before you could get back to tell one of them you've changed your mind.

Glossary

Action: The physical movement within a story, from a fistfight to some-one lifting a teacup and smiling. Whether the action is high- or low-impact, it should be presented as much as possible with concrete and specific language which allows the reader a clear image of the events.

Antagonist: The primary force that stands in the main character's way. In general, protagonists struggle against other people, their environments, or themselves—or against some combination. Beware of thinking of your antagonists as "villains," single-trait characters who are always evil, often for no discernible reason.

Attributive: In dialogue, the phrase which attributes the speech to a given character: "he said," "she asked," "the doctor whined." (*Note:* There is nothing wrong with using the word *said*. Although it is used exten-sively, most readers read over it. Other speech verbs can seem con-trived.)

Backstory: Information about the past which is necessary for the reader to appreciate the present situation or characters. Backstory is presented in one of four forms: dialogue, brief memory, exposition or narration, or flashback.

Beat: A pause in a character's speech for action, description, and/or inter-nal processing. Beats can be used in place of attributives to indicate who is speaking: *"I will not tolerate that man's interference anymore." Davis brought his hand down so hard on the table the silverware jumped. "Take care of him. Now."*

Character: Whoever (or whatever) populates your story. In general, the peo-ple. The primary character is the protagonist, the person who pursues the story goal, and usually the POV. Secondary characters include the antag-onist and those people who perform actions significant to the plot. Tertiary characters are those with whom the protagonist comes in casual contact. Minor characters are those in the background, the people who serve as details on a crowded street, for instance.

Climax: The highest point of tension in the story, the final confrontation of the story's main forces, after which the conflict is decisively resolved and the protagonist's goal is achieved (or not).

Conflict: Two forces in opposition. Cinderella wants to go to the ball, while her stepmother wants her not to and wants one of her own bio-logical daughters to marry the prince. A single woman is trying to adopt a child and has to battle her family and the state. A man fights to recover from the loss of his job. *Narrative tension* is the fear readers have that the protagonist will lose and that the loss will cost dearly. If the villain is too weak or the hero too strong, the victory is too obvious and there is no tension.

Dénouement: Literally, the "unraveling." The dénouement is the passage which wraps up the loose ends after the climax. In most stories, the ending should resolve the conflict neatly enough, either by actual event or by clear suggestion, so that a dénouement is unnecessary. If you feel driven, keep it brief. Remember, after the climax, the story is over.

Description: The sensory information. The idea is to make your scenes so physically vivid that you blur the line between character and reader. By re-creating what comes into the character's senses, you bring the reader into immediate physical contact with the story world. Description is the basic building block of fiction, the one tool you cannot do without.

Dialect: Narration and/or character speech which is written in a distinct regional or ethnic vocabulary and grammatical pattern.

Dialogue: The speech of the people in the story, captured in the words the characters actually use aloud. The idea is to re-create not human speech, but the sense of it. For example, much of what we say in real life is meaningless filler which should be left out of fiction dialogues. *Monologue* is only one person talking, and *interior monologue* is one person sharing thoughts.

Diction: The language level and sentence structure of the prose. Be aware that diction has a profound effect on the tone of your story and, perhaps, an even more profound effect on the way the audience receives the work. Word choices which feel too intellectual and sentences that are too convoluted will make your style seem pompous. Slang and loose sentence structure may make it seem too casual. Diction should be in keeping with the type of story you're writing, the characters you're writing about, and the audience you're writing for. In general, edited English is the choice of writers and readers alike.

Exposition: A relatively objective miniessay which interrupts the story to explain something—a character, a circumstance, a setting. If a story starts in the middle of a piece of action, for example, it is wise to pause briefly fairly early to let the reader know what is going on. Readers like to be intrigued by what is happening in a story, but they don't like to be mystified or confused. You should note that exposition is a nonaction mode, and most readers like action more than essays.

Falling action: See *Rising action.*

Flashback: A passage which has the details and immediacy of a scene, but which clearly takes place prior to the story's present. In other words, the present is put on hold while the past is shown. In general, most of the story should take place in the present frame. If the story is primarily something that takes place in the past, why not set it there to begin with?

Mode: The various types of prose available to a writer: description, action, summary, dialogue, thought, exposition/narration. Each mode moves at a different pace and has its own uses and limitations. For example, dialogue moves faster than exposition/narration, but shouldn't be used to plant blocks of information. Summary covers large blocks of time, but should only be used when nothing truly important is happening. Your choice of mode will be part of your unique style.

Motivation: The reasons your characters act as they do. Every action, no matter how small, has a reason. In most cases, the stimulus/response relationship is so obvious, so reasonable, the action needs no explanation. If the action is too odd, however, you will need to take a little time to keep your reader in credible contact with the character.

Narration: Exposition with an attitude. The sense is that the miniessays come from the narrator (the point-of-view character) instead of from some disembodied, objective voice. The best, and usually the only, guide readers have for how to interpret the events and people is for the character to process things as they happen. As a result, the reader gets not only the information and opinion, but a clearer picture of the narrator's character. Keep your narrator off the soapbox, however.

Narrator: The viewpoint character, the person through whose eyes or over whose shoulder we witness the events and whose nervous system we share. Most often, this is the protagonist, but it is certainly possible to choose a narrator who is simply an observer at a drama about bigger players. In addition, some authors have had success with unreliable narrators, viewpoint characters whose stories can't be trusted.

Omniscience: A specific kind of point of view marked by the ability to know all things everywhere, to read all the character's minds, to see all past and future events at once. While such indulgences were acceptable in early literature, the point of view most acceptable to current readers and editors limits our knowledge to what a single character could know. Even novels, which may switch narrators from time to time, try to maintain a single POV within a given scene or chapter.

Person: A facet of point of view which refers to the relationship between the speaker and the subject:

> First person is *from* the person speaking: "I walked into the room." (*I, we, me, us, my, mine, our*)

> Second person is *to* the person being addressed: "**You** walked into the room." (*you, your*)

Third person is *about* the person being discussed: "**She** walked into the room."*(he, she, it, they, him, her, his, their* as well as names and nouns—*Bob, the dog, armed guards*).

Persona: The mask you put on to tell the story. Even if you write in first person, the narrator is not you, but a character you create.

Plot: The actual cause-and-effect events that resolve the conflict. Plot is the account of the steps the main character takes to reach the goal, the obstacles and the setbacks she encounters on the way, and the measures she takes to overcome them. If the character succeeds, it is *comedy*. If she fails, it is *tragedy*.

Point of view (POV):   The place from which readers view the story, the relative intimacy they have with the main character. Are they inside her head, sharing her senses, her thoughts and emotions? Or are they observing the story's events entirely from the outside like a dispassionate camera. See also *Omniscience* and *Person*.

Protagonist: The main character, the one whose want or need forms the primary story goal and whose journey we follow in pursuit of that goal. Don't confuse *protagonist* with *hero*, who is usually too flawless and one-dimensional to make a character good enough to carry the whole weight of a story.

Rising action: Imagine the story goal as a prize set high in the heavens. As the character makes progress toward the goal, the action is said to "rise." When the character seems to be losing, the movement is away from the goal, or "falling."

Scene: A unit of immediate action and description, shown to us as though we are witnessing it or even taking part, with enough detail so that we can experience it, rather than having it reported to us through summary. Imagine using a telephone to describe an event so well that your listener is able to see, touch, taste, hear, and smell it.

Scene is also used to mean a single unit of time at a single place with a distinct cast of characters. When the time, place, or people change significantly, we start a new scene.

Setting: The sense of the environment in which your story happens. Usually used to mean the sense of place, whether it is large like a country or small like a specific room, setting can also be the historical and social circumstances. Sometimes, the setting can even be the antagonist.

Story: Whether comic or tragic, high-action or parlor drama, a story is the account of the actions a character performs to overcome obstacles in order to obtain a story goal. Both the obstacles and the story goal must be significant to the character, and the resolution satisfying to the reader.

Story goal: What does the main character most want? Most people's goals fall into three broad categories: *reward, relief,* and *revenge.* The specific goal (the type of reward, for example, or the source of misery) is up to the writer, but the story goal should be important enough to the protagonist to give a sense of significant risk if the goal is not reached. Scene goals are smaller, obviously, but the single purpose of any given scene must be to serve the central plot—the pursuit of the story goal.

Stream of consciousness: A narrative technique in which the viewpoint character's observations are presented, not as structured prose, but in the way a mind might actually work—with all its convolutions, impressions, incomplete images, abrupt switchbacks. In its extremes, it is written without grammar, punctuation, or capitalization.

Summary: A generalized report of the events of the story rather than a detailed sensory picture of them. You can summarize characters, emotions, dialogues, and places. Most often, summary is used to compress time, particularly time during which nothing of importance to the story happens. You would not want a novel which takes place over the span of a decade to take ten years to read. The less the physical detail, the more the story tends toward summary.

Symbolism: The use of one object, action, or event to signify another, usually something larger in scope. A beat-up, rusted-out car might represent a whole lifetime of grinding poverty, or angry skies might portend God's displeasure. The idea is to evoke the more significant meaning in the reader's mind without belaboring the point or sounding too moralistic or professorial. The human mind being what it is, virtually anything can be symbolic, from a gesture or a possession to a literary or biblical allusion. Beware of clichés.

Theme: The issue of the story, the point it has to make. In general, it is better to leave such matters to the interpretations of readers and critics. If you feel compelled to have a point, try writing an essay instead. Issues have a way of sacrificing character and plot.

Viewpoint: Six people are affected by an accident, some as witnesses, some as participants. Each will see it differently, each with a different perspective and each with a different set of emotional filters. The one you choose to follow most closely would be the viewpoint character. (See also *Point of View.*)

Index